S P I R I T !

HISTORIC KETCHIKAN, ALASKA

SPIRIT!

HISTORIC KETCHIKAN, ALASKA

Compiled by June Allen

Edited by Patricia Charles

Published by Lind Printing for Historic Ketchikan, Inc.

This book is dedicated to the founders of Ketchikan and their descendants, the Pioneers of Alaska, the Tongass Historical Society, the Tongass Historical Museum and Heritage Center and their staff, and to the people of Ketchikan — past, present and future — who take singular pride in their city and its unique history.

For information, write:

Historic Ketchikan, Inc.
P.O. Box 3364
Ketchikan, Alaska 99901

Cover Design by Sue Ethridge Design
Cover Art by Byron Birdsall (from a Harriet Hunt photograph), loaned by Leif & Tani Stenford, owners of the original, and lifelong Ketchikan residents.

We would like to thank Doug Charles, Museum Registrar, for his invaluable assistance and the Ketchikan Photo Lunch members for generously donating the use of their color transparencies.

Courtesy of Tongass Historical Society

Ketchikan Marching Band, Fourth of July, 1913

This book is intended as a general overview of the history of Ketchikan, compiled from documents, notes, manuscripts, reminiscences, oft-told tales, and historical and contemporary photographs. It is not to be viewed as a text for historical reference. It is designed to be informative and entertaining, a tribute to the spirit of a frontier Alaska town.

TABLE OF CONTENTS

Courtesy of Tongass Historical Society

Photo by U.S. Forest Service

Photo by U.S. Forest Service

Photo by U.S. Forest Service

TABLE OF CONTENTS

Courtesy of Ketchikan Daily News

Courtesy of Ketchikan Daily News

Courtesy of Don "Bucky" Dawson

Courtesy of Tongass Historical Society

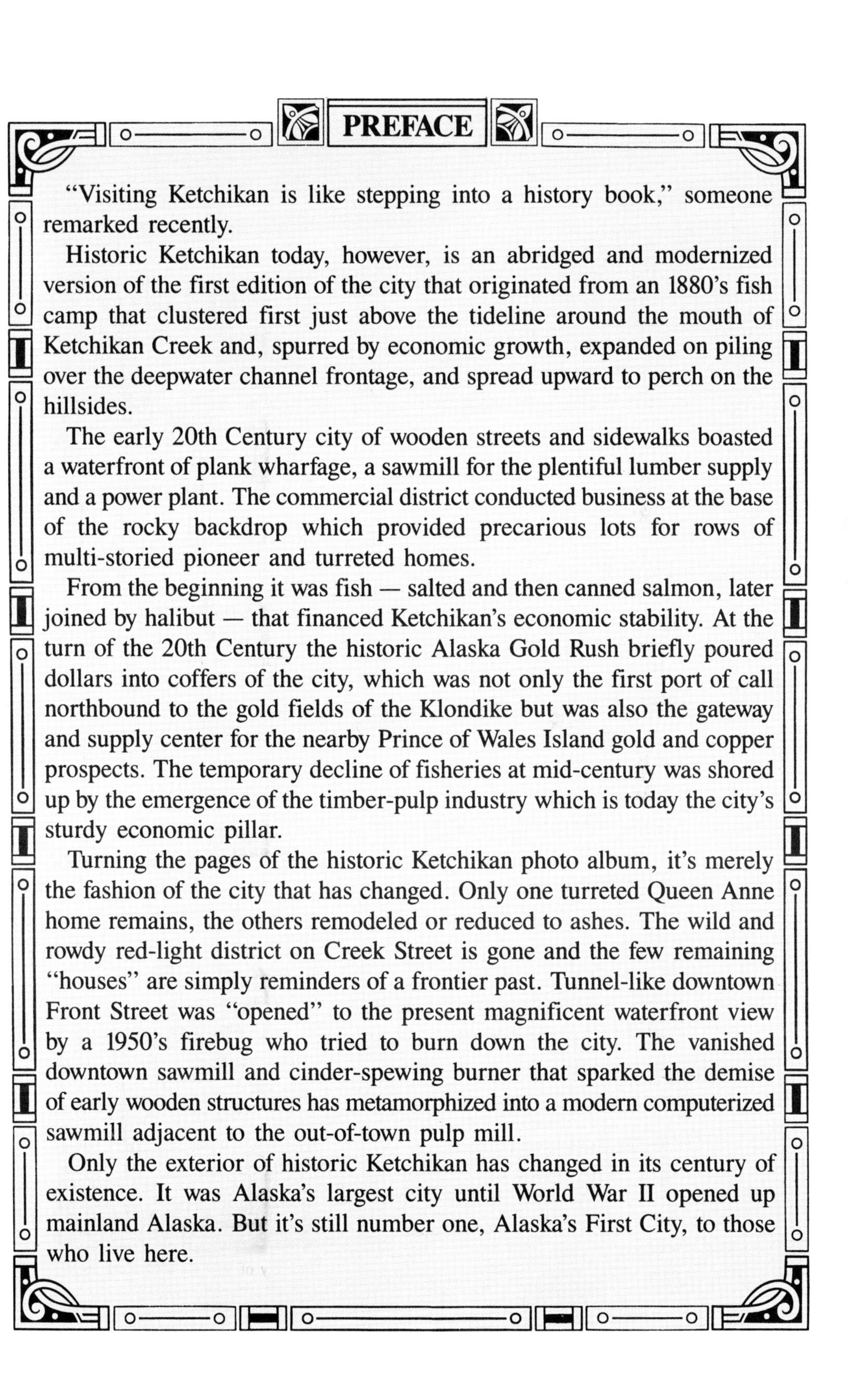

PREFACE

"Visiting Ketchikan is like stepping into a history book," someone remarked recently.

Historic Ketchikan today, however, is an abridged and modernized version of the first edition of the city that originated from an 1880's fish camp that clustered first just above the tideline around the mouth of Ketchikan Creek and, spurred by economic growth, expanded on piling over the deepwater channel frontage, and spread upward to perch on the hillsides.

The early 20th Century city of wooden streets and sidewalks boasted a waterfront of plank wharfage, a sawmill for the plentiful lumber supply and a power plant. The commercial district conducted business at the base of the rocky backdrop which provided precarious lots for rows of multi-storied pioneer and turreted homes.

From the beginning it was fish — salted and then canned salmon, later joined by halibut — that financed Ketchikan's economic stability. At the turn of the 20th Century the historic Alaska Gold Rush briefly poured dollars into coffers of the city, which was not only the first port of call northbound to the gold fields of the Klondike but was also the gateway and supply center for the nearby Prince of Wales Island gold and copper prospects. The temporary decline of fisheries at mid-century was shored up by the emergence of the timber-pulp industry which is today the city's sturdy economic pillar.

Turning the pages of the historic Ketchikan photo album, it's merely the fashion of the city that has changed. Only one turreted Queen Anne home remains, the others remodeled or reduced to ashes. The wild and rowdy red-light district on Creek Street is gone and the few remaining "houses" are simply reminders of a frontier past. Tunnel-like downtown Front Street was "opened" to the present magnificent waterfront view by a 1950's firebug who tried to burn down the city. The vanished downtown sawmill and cinder-spewing burner that sparked the demise of early wooden structures has metamorphized into a modern computerized sawmill adjacent to the out-of-town pulp mill.

Only the exterior of historic Ketchikan has changed in its century of existence. It was Alaska's largest city until World War II opened up mainland Alaska. But it's still number one, Alaska's First City, to those who live here.

Courtesy of Ketchikan Daily News

Courtesy of Don "Bucky" Dawson

LET US INTRODUCE: KETCHIKAN

Ketchikan, Alaska, is a community of some 14,000 residents who work and play like anyone else in spite of an average annual rainfall of more than 160 inches — that's more than 13 feet! It is an isolated island city with no bridges to other islands or to the mainland; its single shore-hugging highway dead ends in the forest 18 miles north of the city limits and 12 miles south. Transportation to Ketchikan is by air or water only.

Ketchikan is located on the rocky southwestern shore of Revillagigedo Island (called Revilla), part of the Alexander Archipelago which makes up most of Alaska's Southeastern Panhandle. Ketchikan is the first port of call northbound into Alaska, and thus its nicknames, "The First City" or "The Gateway City."

On maps and charts, Revilla Island — 35 miles wide and 50 miles long — looks like a floating bite out of the wilderness mainland that encircles most of it. The island is pocked with freshwater lakes and indented with inlets, bays and coves, all of which teem with fish. There are black bear and deer and smaller creatures, and the skies are graced with soaring bald eagles.

When the first white settlers arrived in the 1880s, attracted by hordes of spawning salmon, they saw mountainsides that dropped into the deepwater channel of Tongass Narrows. There was only one exception, the sloping beach carved at the mouth of Ketchikan Creek. Here was the first industry, a fish saltery. On the deepwater shoreline that arched westward, the pioneers drove piling and capped and decked them to create a wooden city on stilts.

Twenty-foot tides moved in to lap at foundations of buildings perched on solid rock at the edge of the decked town. As time passed, the city's watery basement was gradually filled with rock and dredged materials. No longer could boats tie up at the foot of St. John's Church on Mission Street. But today, as then, the surge of full moon high tides slips in under downtown buildings to puddle basement floors.

It was this salt water, home to rich varieties of marine life, that gave Ketchikan its fisheries foothold on: "the rock"; it was the heavy precipitation that created the magnificent rain forest providing timber for later development and economic security. And it is its magnificent scenery, hospitality and envied lifestyles that bring visitors to see and experience it.

Ketchikan has only two traffic lights. There is no "fast food strip." The average age of the seniors in the Pioneers Home is 89. It is a healthy place to live. It is a quiet town with little crime. But it was not always so. Ketchikan has a shady past, a comfortable present and perhaps a shining future. This is its story. This is Ketchikan, Alaska.

Photo by Schallerer/Tongass Historical Society

Ketchikan Boat Parade, July 4, 1940

DISCOVERY AND PURCHASE

The Explorers' Tale

Captain James Cook was the international hero of his day. Three times he set sail from England on voyages of exploration of the Pacific Rim. Even during the American Revolution, his ship as it crossed the Atlantic was safe from enemy guns. Unfortunately, Captain Cook met an untimely end in 1779 at age 51 at the hands of Hawaiian Island natives. His exploratory routes were followed more than a decade later by the more precise English cartographer and cataloguer, Captain George Vancouver.

It was Vancouver who, ignoring or being unable to pronounce or spell aboriginal names already in existence, (had he taken the trouble to learn them), bestowed names on many of Southeast Alaska's major geographical features — waterways, the larger islands, capes and points. All are good, solid English names, many honoring English nobility. The spectacular eastern reaches of Behm Canal which separates Revilla Island from the mainland must have been as awesome to Vancouver as it is to today's visitors to Misty Fiords National Monument. He named the volcanic core of Behm Canal landmark New Eddystone Rock because of its resemblance to the lighthouse on Eddystone in the English Channel off Plymouth.

But Captain Vancouver's voyages of exploration near what today is called Ketchikan were not without incident. It was 1793. Vancouver had not forgotten what happened to his predecessor James Cook at the hands of frightened or unfriendly Hawaiian natives. At a cove on the northwest shoulder of Revillagigedo Island — after circumnavigating the island — he sent ashore a survey party in an open boat. It was attacked by a party of natives who had pretended to be friendly. Two of Vancouver's men were wounded by spears. So he named the bay Traitors Cove and the adjacent prominence Escape Point. Closer to Ketchikan, he named Betton Island after one of the wounded.

The still remote islands of Southeast Alaska still carry names given by early explorers, some remembered, some origins forgotten.

The Three Georges

It was the era of the three Georges in 1793. President George Washington was in the final year of his first term. The taxing George III of England would occupy his throne for another quarter of a century, bemoaning the loss of the American Colonies. Captain George Vancouver charted, in

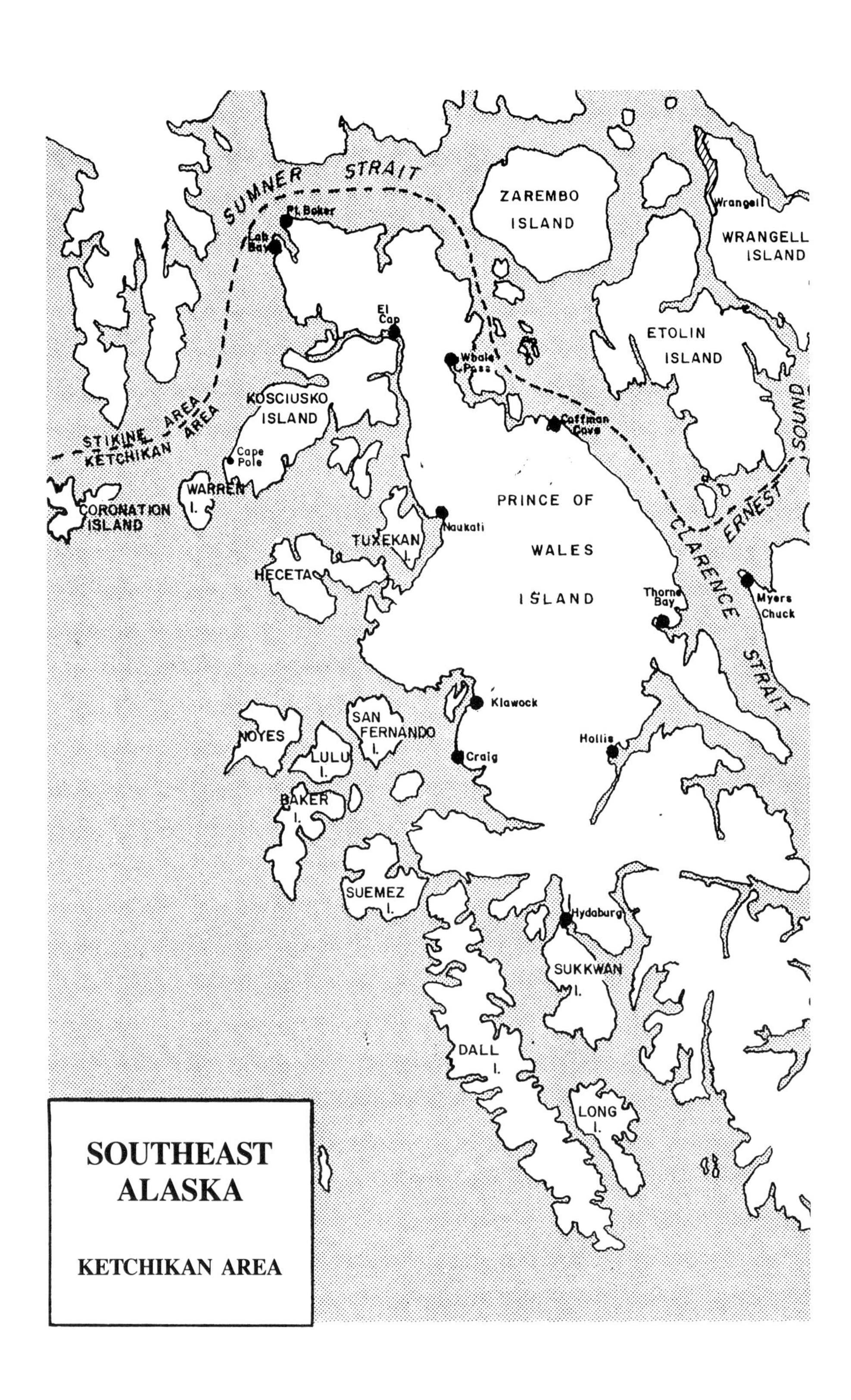
SUMNER STRAIT
ZAREMBO ISLAND
Wrangell
WRANGELL ISLAND
Pt. Baker
El Cap
Whale Pass
ETOLIN ISLAND
KOSCIUSKO ISLAND
Coffman Cove
STIKINE AREA
KETCHIKAN AREA
Cape Pole
WARREN I.
CORONATION ISLAND
PRINCE OF WALES ISLAND
Naukati
TUXEKAN I.
HECETA
ERNEST SOUND
CLARENCE STRAIT
Thorne Bay
Myers Chuck
Klawock
Craig
Hollis
NOYES
SAN FERNANDO I.
LULU I.
BAKER I.
SUEMEZ I.
Hydaburg
SUKKWAN I.
DALL I.
LONG I.
SOUTHEAST ALASKA
KETCHIKAN AREA

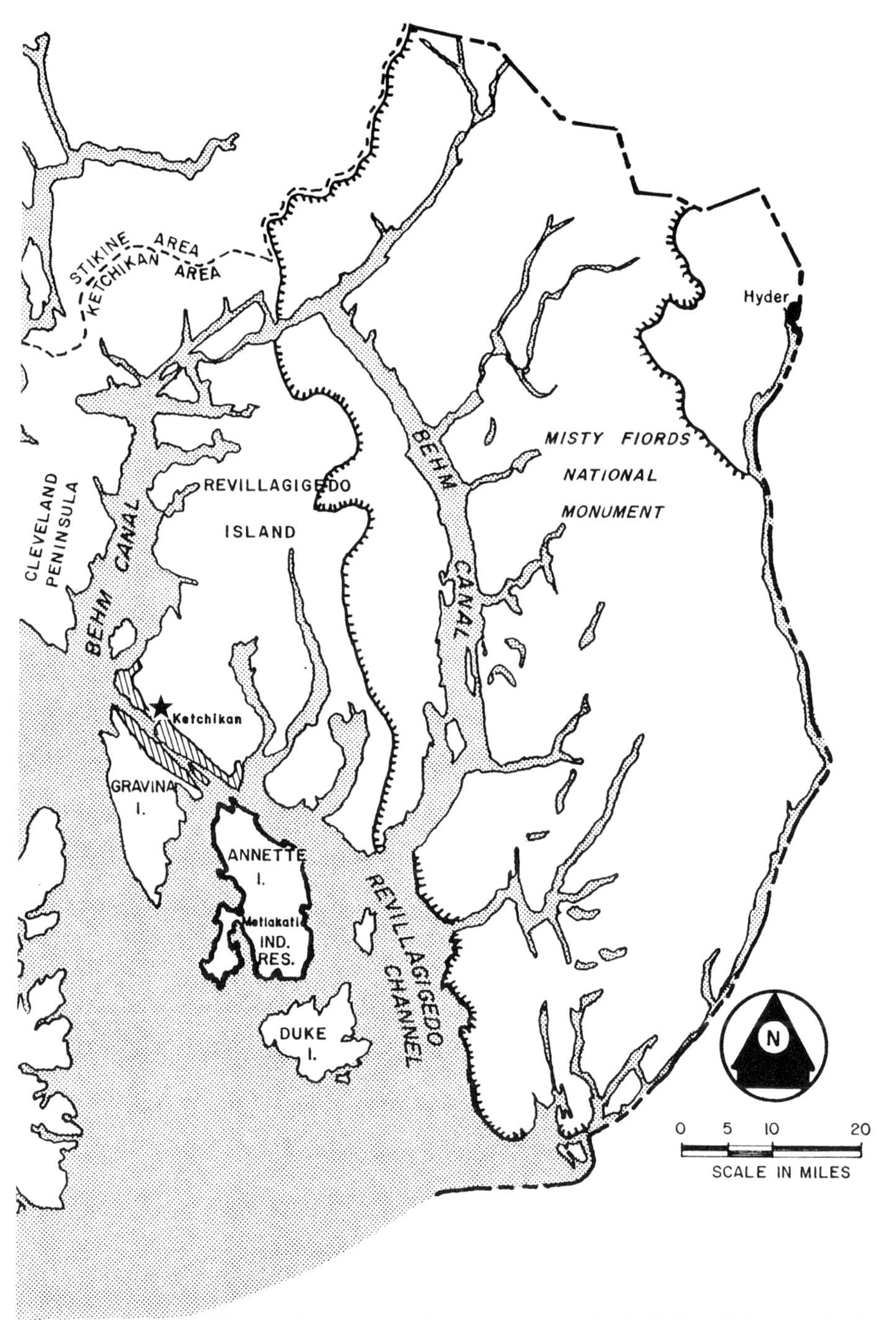

This map is reproduced from maps prepared by the USDA, U.S. Forest Service

that year of 1793, the significant features of the 1,168-square-mile island which today is edged, along its southwest face, by today's Ketchikan.

Vancouver named this island Revillagigedo, extending to the island the Spanish-bestowed name of the Inside Passage channel which leads to it. The channel had been named just a year earlier by Spanish explorer Jacinto Caamano for Don Juan Vicente de Guemes Pacheco de Padilla Horcasitas, count of Revilla Gigedo and Viceroy of Mexico. Or, as a long-gone sign near Ketchikan's seaplane airport used to say, "Or something like that."

Today's residents call their island a more simple "Revilla."

In spite of the flurry of multi-national exploratory activity in this rich new northern territory in the waning years of the 18th century, no new claims would be made. England's Hudson's Bay Company had reached as far west in Canada as it could politically go. Russia had her secure and proprietary interest in several strategic locations stretching east-west in the North Pacific from Siberia to Sitka and Wrangell, and vaguer, unfortified claims to the entire fur-rich chain of islands lining the underarm of the North American continent's Pacific shoulder.

Aware of but undaunted by the incursion of explorer interests in their land, the aboriginal Indian tribes of these southernmost reaches closest to the Pacific West Coast of the expanding United States continued their centuries-old lifestyles. They wintered at permanent villages in sheltered locales and summered at fish camps at the mouths of salmon-rich streams within their traditional territories.

One of those fish camps was at what would become known as Ketchikan Creek on Revilla Island, a narrow white-water stream that rushes over shining boulders to empty into an estuary that waxes and wanes with 20-foot tides. Schools of pink salmon can be trusted to return each year to obey their instincts to jump the challenging rocky rapids to their spawning grounds upstream.

After the U.S. Purchase of Alaska from Russia in 1867, there arose financial interests in this curious northern territory that continue to this day.

National fishery interests began to explore the potential of the newly acquired northern resources and sent out agents to establish locations for processing. These started out as salmon salteries as early as 1878 with the first operation at Klawock, on Prince of Wales Island. Salteries were operational at the infant communities of Ketchikan and Loring, located some twenty miles north, within a year of each other, probably 1883-1884.

Loring, with a cannery and post office by 1885, was expected to become the "city" and Ketchikan the satellite. However, as salteries graduated into canneries with heavy packs of fish, Ketchikan's more salubrious mainline shipping location, harbor and weather won out over Loring's turn-again water route and winds.

Ketchikan is documented as becoming a commercial center, therefore a bona fide town, in 1887. That was also the year that Father William Duncan led his band of Tsimshian Indians from Canada to Alaska to found Metlakatla. It was the year that the missionary after whom Saxman Indian village is named was lost at sea while looking for a townsite.

By 1900 the fever of the Gold Rush of '98 had cooled. The hardiest of prospectors were stampeding elsewhere or heading home. Some stopped in Ketchikan for supplies to prospect on Prince of Wales Island. Ketchikan grew. It was the opening year of the new Twentieth Century that Ketchikan became a city.

The Tale of Tongass Island

Long before the first European explorers, adventurers and American entrepreneurs sailed into Alaska waters, the Tongass tribe of Tlingit Indians lived on Tongass Island, located near the mouth of Portland Canal. This deepwater fjord, sixty miles long and a mile to a mile and a half in width, cuts into the mainland through spectacular scenery, the most scenic near its island-choked mouth. In summer the water erupts with the rust-colored bodies of sporting sea lions and sparkles silver with the jumping, twisting bodies of spawning salmon.

When American soldiers arrived on Tongass Island in 1868 to build a fort, shortly after the 1867 U.S. Purchase of Alaska from Russia, they lived close by the Tongass village Tlingits. Prospectors, adventurers and traders sometimes called at the island, as did the supply and mail boats stopping at the fort. But within two years the fort was abandoned, leaving the Tongass villagers once again alone on their island.

Then in 1869 William Seward, Secretary of State who was instrumental in the Purchase of Alaska, toured the new northern domain. He was invited to a gala potlatch in his honor at Tongass village. Potlatch gifts were given to the American dignitary, who unfortunately didn't understand that he was expected to return the compliment.

So Tongass Chief Ebbitts commissioned a totem pole to be carved in remembrance of the notable visit. It is called the Seward totem pole and stands today near the community house in Saxman's Totem Park. The Seward pole is a shame pole, for the politician's failure to respect the customs of his hosts.

Courtesy of the Royal British Columbia Museum, Victoria, B.C.

Tongass Village

Fort Tongass: 1868

October 18, 1867: The Russian Bear comes down and the Stars and Stripes go up the flagpole in the parade grounds at Sitka, capital of Russian-America, as ceremonies complete the Transfer of Alaska from Russia to the purchaser, the United States of America.

April 29, 1868: Fort Tongass is established under special orders of the U.S. Military Division of the Pacific. Described as of "temporary character," the fort on Tongass Island consists of buildings made of logs, "ceiled within and weather-boarded without." There is no stockade. The buildings are not positioned with reference to each other and therefore are not effective for defense of the compound — if it should come to that.

Today there is little to be seen at the site on the shore of Tongass Island some 40 miles south of Ketchikan other than a sandy beach, suitable for beaching small boats, and a level clearing behind. Fort Tongass was abandoned in 1870. There also is little to be seen of the village of the Tongass tribe of some 200 Tlingit Indians who shared their island for two years with the Americans. In 1894 the Tongass Indians followed missionaries to a new village just south of the infant city of Ketchikan.

But in 1868, when orders established the fort, it was seen as necessary to protect American interests in the raw new country. Fort Tongass was just eight miles northwest of the southernmost international boundary between Canada and Alaska, and twelve miles north of the Hudson's Bay post at Fort Simpson, Canada, with its large village of some 2,000 Tsimshian Indians. Fort Tongass was established "to prevent smuggling and other illicit trade with the Indians and to preserve peace between the British and American tribes trading and fishing in the vicinity of Portland Canal."

To preserve the peace, Fort Tongass originally was to have been garrisoned by Battery E, 2nd Artillery, Captain C.H. Pierce commanding

Courtesy of Tongass Historical Society

Fort Tongass

five commissioned officers and one hundred and three enlisted men. There were to be two Napoleon guns and four mountain howitzers. Before the men were unpacked, on May 8, 1868, two of those officers and fifty-one of those men under the command of Lieutenant John H. Smith were sent to Fort Wrangell to establish a post there. They took with them one of the Napoleons and two of the howitzers.

Fort Wrangell, the earlier Russian fur-trading outpost Fort Dionysius, was some 130 miles northwest of Fort Tongass. It guarded the mouth of the Stikine River from the mainland, a river which Canada's Hudson's Bay traders traveled to slip into Russian, then American, territory to trade with the Stikine Indians. (The international boundary between Alaska and Canada allowed the latter no ports north of Fort Simpson.)

Thus, with Fort Tongass and Fort Wrangell in place, new American trading and commercial interests were protected from competition with their Canadian counterparts.

There apparently was little to protect at Fort Tongass. There was no warfare between the Tlingits and the Tsimshians during those years. Hudson's Bay traders made no overt moves into American territory. For the soldiers it was a life of isolation and inactivity. That was fortunate, because the fort on Tongass Island was hastily erected, poorly garrisoned and ill-equipped with a store of ammunition that didn't fit the arms of the troops. The men received mail once a month from a ship on the regular run between Portland, Oregon, and the Alaska capital at Sitka, and occasionally via the irregular government supply steamers. For newspapers the men depended on British ships and Hudson's Bay sources as well. (So much for rivalry.)

By June of 1870 the force at Fort Tongass had been reduced to 42 men. As expirations of terms of service came up, no replacements were sent. Abandonment was ordered. Left behind were the kitchen and mess quarters, the barracks, unfinished officers' quarters, an unfinished hospital, and a storeroom choked with building supplies never used.

All that remains of Fort Tongass today are the reports of a tired Army Lieutenant Caziaro, disappointed by the abandonment of the fort and yet ready to leave. Today, if the tides are right, the Alaska state ferry Aurora glides past Tongass Island on summer voyages to and from Hyder at the head of the Portland Canal.

THE FIRST INHABITANTS

The First Four Women

Is the complex family structure of the Alaska Indian peoples a clue to their beginnings or their arrival in the New World from Asia thousands of years ago? Who were those first arrivals?

Alaska's Tlingit Indians are divided into two phratries, or "main families," the Wolf and the Raven. The Haida Indians have two phratries, the Raven and the Eagle. The Tsimshians, however, have four — the Bear, the Wolf, the Raven and the Eagle. A phratry consists of a number of clans, or, smaller family units. Within any of the tribes, a member cannot marry within his own phratry or clan.

In custom, all three tribes are matriarchal. That is, descent is traced through the mother's line, and all children belong to the mother's phratry and clan. Parents do not make the decisions about a child's rearing; that is the job of an uncle, the mother's brother. The son of a clan chief would not ordinarily inherit his father's position; that usually would go to a son of a chief's sister.

Men are the titular heads of the clan families, but sometimes a woman might lead her family. A log of Captain Vancouver's and other early explorers' voyages tell of canoes approaching ships, with women leaders in the bow.

Women were the historians, passing on to their daughters and granddaughters the stories of their clan and phratry families. Working together to gather and prepare food allowed ample time for passing on family history. During leisure time around lodge fires in the winters, the men passed on the legends and heroic tales learned from their fathers, uncles and grandfathers.

With the Southeastern Alaska Indians, as with the Eskimos to the north, the various words in each tongue used to describe themselves translated generally into "The People." And within the oral histories of each of the tribes were stories of their earliest times, which might be interpreted as stretching back to a crossing of the Bering Sea Land Bridge from Asia into Alaska.

Until now, all political (as in the Alaska Native Claims Settlement Act of 1971) and most scientific grouping of Native peoples has been made on the basis of language. However, new genetic and DNA studies may modify that.

Courtesy of Washington State Historical Society

Metlakatla

A study conducted at Emory University in Atlanta, Georgia, states that nearly all American Indians from Alaska to South America are descendants of a small band of pioneers who crossed the Land Bridge somewhere between 15,000 and 30,000 years ago. The exceptions are the Navajos and Apaches and the Eskimos and Aleuts (the Alaska Athabaskans were not mentioned), who arrived later.

The information came from a study of American Indians' mitochondrial genes, which are energy producing genes separate from the body's other genes. They are passed to children only through the mother, not the father. Grouping showed that those American Indians tested were descendants of only four women.

Is it possible that the first band of pioneer migrants were Tsimshians — who alone of Alaska's Indians have four phratries — descendants of the families of the first four women?

(Information for this story came from Pauline Williams, who is a Tsimshian of the Wolf phratry, and who has passed on to her daughters her clan's oral history learned from her mother and grandmother.)

Photo by Schallerer/Courtesy of Laurie Coates

Father Duncan's Church interior, Metlakatla

Metlakatla: One Man's Mission

Perhaps no tale of courage and faith is better known in Southeastern Alaska than the story of Father William Duncan's mission to the Tsimshian Indians. Duncan was a lay Anglican missionary sent from England to Canada in 1857 to minister to the Tsimshians at their village at Fort Simpson.

Fort Simpson was a Hudson's Bay post on the southern shore of the entrance to Portland Canal, four miles south of the boundary between Russian-America (at the time) and Canada. Tribes of Tsimshians from the Nass and Skeena River areas, numbering an estimated 3,000, had congregated around the fort. Their village was described as having at least 100 lodges, each of which was thirty to forty feet wide, sixty feet long and fifteen to twenty feet in height.

When Duncan arrived in 1857 he was greeted by what he called "savagery and bloodshed." He immediately set out to learn the language of his flock and when this was accomplished, he visited each Tsimshian home and took a census. While visiting, he aroused their curiosity about his God and his teachings. It was Duncan's courage and faith that kept him at a task that was very nearly impossible when all he taught could be undone by the influence of a jealous shaman or a cask of liquor.

To move his people from the temptations of "civilization," Duncan decided in 1862 to resettle the faithful and dependable of his flock in a new home seventeen miles south of the fort, at what they named Metlakatla. Six canoes with about fifty Tsimshians set out for their new home.

The schoolhouse from Fort Simpson was rafted to the new community. The flock began to plant and gather food for the coming winter. Over the twenty-five years of "old" Metlakatla's existence, more and more of the Tsimshians from Fort Simpson followed, willing to abide by Duncan's rules. These included a list of religious duties and observances and the pledge to give up alcohol, deviltry and gambling. The community grew and prospered.

Duncan's unprecedented methods — offering his own slightly revised religious instruction plus employment skills — caused friction with church leaders in England. He decided to move his people out of Canada and out of the reach of the organized church and into what had become a U.S. possession, Alaska. He received permission from the U.S. Government to do so.

He and his followers scouted locations for a "new" Metlakatla farther north, and chose a former Tlingit village site at Port Chester, on the west

Courtesy of Tongass Historical Society

First hotel in Metlakatla

Courtesy of Tongass Historical Society

Father Duncan, Metlakatla

coast of Annette Island. In 1887 a band went ahead to begin building and planting. The American flag was raised August 7 of that year. Father Duncan remained alertly political and in 1891 the community gained U.S. Indian reservation status.

Duncan understood human nature as well as the temperament of his flock. The town was laid out with four homesites to a block, so that everyone could have a corner lot. He encouraged the planting of gardens and flowers. If his people found fault with him, it was because he jealously guarded his complete control of community affairs.

As a businessman as well as a minister of God, Duncan believed that for any people to be strong and prosperous, the community itself must be strong and self-supporting. The Tsmshians built a cannery, stores, a sawmill and their impressive church. Indian agents and missionaries around the world followed the progress of his work.

Father Duncan died in 1918 and was buried on the east side of the church. His monument is decorated with a hand holding high a burning torch. The Tsimshians chose that emblem because it signified "He brought us the light." In 1923 his grave was visited by President Warren G. Harding who laid a wreath on his grave.

Photo by U.S. Forest Service

Metlakatla

Life in a Haida Village

By Albert J. Brown, Sr.

When I was a youngster in the early 1920s I used to look forward to the annual trip my mother and dad took to gather the black seaweed that occurs in only three weeks of the year and only on shorelines exposed to the open sea. Our trips were usually to Cape Muzon where there were old campsites and lots of clean beaches on which to dry the seaweed. Other families did the same thing, so for a few days the old camp had the air of a resort.

On the way to Cape Muzon we had to pass by the old abandoned Haida village of Howkan, so either on the way out or on the way back the old folks would stop and explore. We kids would run the village site from one end to the other. At that time there were a few of the old buildings still standing — the church and manse, and one of the old homes that had been built before the village was abandoned. There were also corner posts of the community houses and the totem poles that had stood at the entrances, and the old carved eagle in the center of the village plus many grave sites with totem markers still standing.

There was plenty of nostalgia to savor and we couldn't help but wonder how things used to be before our culture was corrupted by civilization. How did they get along without the musket, metal tools, cloth? What did they carry water in, how did they preserve food without salt and refrigeration? Actually, there is much evidence that they made out very well.

Before metal tools they had stone implements — axes, wedges, spear heads, arrow heads, stone knives and stone mashers. There is no way of knowing when the Indians first acquired metal tools. There are ancient legends telling that if a man wanted to find a drift log with a piece of metal in it, he'd fast for so many days and make medicine before he started

Photo by Harriet Hunt/Tongass Historical Society

Howkan Village

looking. The Pacific Rim covers a vast area of the world, including China with its sophisticated culture two thousand years in advance of Europe. It's not unreasonable to speculate that the Indians may have acquired metal before the arrival of the trading schooners. The Indians already knew about copper by trading with Interior Indians, so they had some knowledge of metal. Even today you find drift logs that appear to have come from the Orient, with carvings of oriental style.

Most villages were located near fresh spring water because Indians had an aversion to drinking from salmon streams. To carry water they wove baskets of spruce roots so closely knit that they held water. To waterproof, they would line the basket with pitch.

To preserve food they devised methods of dehydration. Dried salmon is the most familiar product. Add a little smoke and you have a product in common use today. Meat of all kinds — deer, sea lion or seal — was treated the same way. The meat was precooked by boiling, then dry-smoked in small pieces. After that it was put into containers of hooligan grease oil, seal oil or even tallow from deer. Believe me, this is good!

Everyone knows about bent cedar boxes. The large ones with elaborate designs were used to store blankets, beads and ceremonial robes. Less attention is paid to the smaller boxes, about a foot-and-a-half square and two feet high that were used for storing food. They too were decorated but with less elaborate designs. The Haida name for them was "towt," almost like the English word "tote."

It was with these boxes in mind that the early Indians dried the seaweed. They made square frames that would fit inside the towt. The frames were laid down and filled with the fresh seaweed, then dried in the sun. The frames were turned until the seaweed was completely dry, resulting in a square seaweed pad about three-quarters of an inch thick. These were stacked into the wooden boxes without any waste space.

Berries were prepared in the same manner as seaweed. Berries were mashed until most of the juice was gone, then put into frames and dried in the sun. The square pads were stored in boxes for winter use. Stone instruments shaped like a T with wider pads at the end were used for mashing berries. In the winter the berries were broken in pieces, mixed with snow and a little oil and then whipped into a pink froth — an excellent ice cream.

Those days are gone. I was talking to my father-in-law who visited old Howkan not too long ago. There had been a sandspit in the bay which was the playground of Haida children for many, many generations. He says the last earthquake took away the sandspit. But there are no children to play there now, in the abandoned village.

(Albert J. Brown, Sr. was born in Howkan in 1911, a member of the Raven clan of the Haida tribe. He writes that he is "half Norwegian and half Haida Indian, the better half being Indian.")

Northward Bound

The Queen Charlotte Island group, off the coast of British Columbia, is the ancestral home of the Haida Indians. Scientific sources suggest that the Haida people crossed the Bering Land Bridge into Alaska, west to east, thousands of years ago. Some Haidas disagree. They say they have always been here and their migrations have been south to north.

There is at least one Haida legend that tells of a tropical, Polynesian-like homeland. Could the people have traveled north with continental drift? Or did they migrate from Polynesia to Asia and thence to the Bering Land Bridge?

Stories vary as to when and why some of the Haida left the Queen Charlottes some 200 years ago to settle farther north, in what today is Alaska. Possibly population increases simply strained the islands' resources. One story says the break came after a clan quarrel over a salmon stream. Another says children were shooting drying salmon from the racks of each other's families, began to quarrel and soon pulled their elders into a much larger quarrel which led to several factions' packing up and moving north.

One version of the migration says the Haida moved into abandoned Tlingit villages on Prince of Wales Island, burned the old structures and built anew. Another account says that the Haida were able, fearsome warriors who drove the Tlingits out. The villages the Haida founded are said to be Howkan, Klinkwan, Dakoo, Sukkwan and Hetta. In any event, the newcomers, called the Kaigani Haida, chose locations that put their new villages close to the busy Pacific trade routes of the 19th century.

Courtesy of Tongass Historical Museum

Sukkwan Village

The Haida people were taller and of fairer skin than their Tlingit and Tsimshian neighbors. They were recognized as the most creative of the carvers. They had learned to make huge canoes from the giant cedar that grew conveniently near the water's edge of their islands. Some of their canoes were said to be as long as the sailing ships of the explorers. And they were skilled boatmen, having to travel from the Queen Charlottes across forty miles of rough water to reach the mainland where they had traded with the Tsimshians of the Nass River for ooligan grease and soapberries.

The sizeable Haida village of Howkan was well established at the turn of the 20th century when the U.S. Government and Christian missionaries began to take an interest in Alaska's Native people. The village was appropriately decorated with totem poles — carved cedar "books" and "memorials" of their culture. In the center of the village was the magnificent Eagle totem.

In 1911 the Bureau of Indian Affairs resettled Haida villagers in new communities of Hydaburg and Kasaan, with schools and churches, leaving

Photo by Harriet Hunt/Tongass Historical Society

Klinquan Village, 1906

behind totem poles and community houses. Twenty-seven years later, in 1938, the Hydaburg cannery was built, providing employment. In 1964 it closed. It reopened in 1971 and operated — with only a short closure in 1980 — until it was destroyed by fire in 1984. The Haidas still fish for a living.

Today Hydaburg is a town of about 400 and Kasaan numbers about 50.

A Haida Tale

Haida Indians, wrote Haida chronicler Albert J. Brown, Sr., have always had a spiritual affinity with the killer whale, equating the whales' clan system of obedience and loyalty to their own. The relationship is strengthened by the fact that no legend recounts an attack by a killer whale on a human. In fact, Haida stories tell of the whales helping men struggling in the water.

One legend tells of a woodcutter named Dooni who drowned after overloading his canoe, which was swamped in a squall. Dooni then becomes conscious of "beings" inviting him to join them. He accompanies them to a village where he enters a community house and, after discussion, is adopted by them. When a dorsal fin is selected for him he realizes these are killer whales he has joined. He feels the heated fin bind to his back and then he sees them as whales.

He travels with the pod but becomes homesick, and reluctant permission is granted for him to return to his village, where he is left on the beach. He sees his old community house and eagerly runs to it. Once inside he greets his relatives but no one can see or hear him, because he is in the spiritual world. Outside, he finds rainwater dripping from the eaves and sits under it. Slowly the dripping water peels off his spirit life.

He returns to the house and is greeted by his incredulous relatives. After happy greetings, he tells his story. And now his people know that those lost at sea are often adopted spiritually into the killer whale pod.

The Story of Saxman

Tongass village on Tongass Island near the mouth of Portland Canal south of Ketchikan was "discovered," at least in official documentation, in 1868 when the U.S. Army, assigned as guardians of newly purchased Alaska, constructed a fort there less than a year after the Purchase.

Army officers described the Tlingit community as "a village of some 200 expert boatmen, shrewd and successful traders friendly to whites." Their lodges were described as constructed with great skill by rough adzes and arranged with ingenuity to shelter twenty-five to thirty people each. The U.S. soldiers said, however, that the Tongass people were poorly armed with flintlock guns which they purchased from (the competitive) Hudson's Bay at $15 apiece — but which they kept in excellent order. The fort was abandoned and the last of the soldiers departed only two years after arriving.

Anthropologists suggest the Tongass and Cape Fox Indians had lived on their islands for generations before the incursion of the European explorers, the subsequent trading with the Russian "owners" of their lands, and the ultimate occupation of their island by the U.S. Army. Information gathered from the oral history of the elders indicated that in the distant past the Tongass people had migrated to their location near the mouth

Photo by G.T. Emmons/Royal British Columbia Museum, Victoria, B.C.

Halibut House, Saxman, 1889

of Portland Canal from the Northwest coast of Prince of Wales Island.

Before they had ever seen a white man, they had already suffered his presence from afar, falling victim to an epidemic of smallpox originating with the Russian settlers farther north in Kodiak and Sitka. In 1862 their numbers were again diminished during another epidemic of the same disease believed to have spread westward across the continent and north through Alaska. In 1869, as the U.S. soldiers were leaving, the Tongass numbered 500.

At that time their chief was Andah, a venerable leader with snow-white hair. He had adopted in earlier years the name of Ebbits from the captain of some ship that had visited his island, a man he admired. Before his death, he had a great totem pole erected and on a tablet near it was later inscribed, "To the memory of Ebbits, Head Chief of the Tongass, who died in 1880, aged 100 years."

The chief's son was called Kinnanook, perhaps named for an early chief

Courtesy of Tongass Historical Society

Saxman

of the Tlingit, who is said to have directed one of the first white explorers away from his own people and toward the fierce Haida of the Queen Charlotte Islands as the source of "great numbers of sea otter skins and robes."

In 1886, a young Presbyterian minister, Samuel A. Saxman, and his wife, Margaret, arrived at Tongass village to teach school. They learned that the people of Tongass and Cape Fox villages were interested in combining into one village at a new place suitable for a school. While in search of a site, Saxman and several Native companions drowned.

By 1890, the Tongass numbered only 225. In 1894 the two tribes made the long-planned move and settled on the shore above a small cove just three miles south of Ketchikan. The village on Tongass Island quickly fell to ruins, although twenty-four totem poles were left behind. Some of those fell prey to "scientific expeditions" studying the Northwest Indian cultures.

Settled in their new home on Revillagigedo Island near the infant city of Ketchikan, the Tongass and Cape Fox Indians named the new community Saxman, after their lost missionary. A Presbyterian mission school opened in 1895, headed by James W. Young, who not only taught classes but preached as well. He helped the people form a town government.

The Saxman Tlingits buried their dead on Pennock Island across Tongass Narrows from their village. Today the graveyard is largely abandoned. There is said to be one unusual headstone still in good repair, a pair of bears guarding the final resting place of a chief.

By 1912 more and more of the Tlingits had moved from Saxman to Ketchikan, accessible only by boat, to take advantage of seasonal job opportunities in the booming frontier town. Most returned to Saxman for the winter months. Of the 300 or so who had settled Saxman originally, not enough were left in the village year-round to conduct regular services, so church activities moved to the more active churches in Ketchikan and Metlakatla. In 1925 a road was built to connect Saxman with Ketchikan and the Tlingits in Ketchikan began to move back to their own community.

In the mid-1930s, during the Great Depression, the Civilian Conservation Corps (CCC) built Saxman's beautiful Totem Park. Totem poles from the abandoned villages and cemeteries of Tongass and Cape Fox sites, and Cat, Village and Pennock Islands, were brought to Saxman and installed in the new park. A Community House now stands in the park behind a semi-circle of totem poles, including the famous Lincoln and Secretary of State poles, both brought from Tongass village. Saxman village and its Totem Park are favorite stops for Ketchikan's many visitors.

Recently the Cape Fox Indian Corporation built a new hotel atop Boston Smith hill, with a tramway to carry guests up the cliff behind Creek Street. The hotel is designed in the spirit of an original Tlingit community house and is graced with elegant Tlingit carving and totem poles.

A Potlatch Prank

Many years ago a steamer trunk which had never been claimed was finally cleared from a storage facility in Ketchikan. Papers inside indicated that the trunk had belonged to a former schoolteacher who was never traced, so the trunk could not be returned. The teacher had worked at the Indian school on Deermount Street, back in the days sometime before Alaska schools were desegregated in 1947.

The teacher had collected old stories from the parents of his pupils.

Courtesy of Tongass Historical Society

Bear Totem, Pennock Island

The stories were typed on onion skin paper and filed in a folder. This is the story one Tlingit father related to the teacher:

"My father went to a potlatch on Tongass Island many, many years ago. It was about 1890 or 1891, I think. A potlatch is a big party. A man must be very rich to give a potlatch. We don't have potlatches much anymore. Nobody rich enough. If someone give me deerskin nowadays, I probably say 'Phuii!' And nobody going to give me a slave, huh?

"But at this potlatch, it was on Tongass Island a long time ago, my father said, there were many people from the islands around here. The two chiefs had many gifts to give. There were also five or maybe six white men there. For six days the people ate and gambled, ate some more and then exchanged gifts. There was much merrymaking, much fun.

"Then there was a show put on. Three parts to this old show. First was a shadow show just for us Indians, for our own amusement. A sail from one of our canoes was stretched across the room and behind it candles and lamps. The people made some funny shadows on that sail! Then there was another part, also just for us, when the medicine man, I guess you could call him, show us how to make medicine on a man's eyes. He took those eyes out of that man's head and put them back in again! Amazing!

"Then the third part was for the guests who was white men. There was a knocking at the door and the chief called 'Come in!' But nothing happened. The knock came again and once more the chief called 'Come in!', louder this time. But no one came through the door. Then there came another knock and the chief cried out, angry now, 'Come in!' But no one heard him. So the chief went to the door and pulled in a big bird with a long neck and white head.

"This white head bobbed all around and looked all over the room but didn't see anything or anyone he knew. The Indians all laughed and held their sides, but the bird just stared. The six white men laughed, too, and all the people looked out the corners of their eyes at them, to see if they knew why they were laughing.

"You see the joke? The bird was the white man, too dumb to come in the door, not knowing anyone, not understanding the Indian way."

Monuments in Cedar

One of Ketchikan's main attractions is its collection of totem poles, the largest in the world — some 113 monuments in cedar. In two totem parks and in other public locations in or near the city are 86 poles; there are also 27 totem poles owned by private parties. Some of the totem poles have been crafted recently by Native carvers and ceremoniously raised; others are almost a century old and are being carefully protected against further decay.

Totem poles are more than symbolic records of events, families and traditional stories — they are also marvels of creative art and engineering skills. After the various totemic symbols were carved on cedar logs and painted, the huge poles were raised and set into the earth with ingenious rope rigging and manpower, without mechanical aids. And many of these totem poles withstood gale-force winds to stand upright after nearby community houses in abandoned villages had fallen into decay.

Totem poles are made up of a series of crests which represent objects, animals, people and supernatural beings, representing clans. It isn't possible to "read" a totem pole, because the complete story would be known only to the owner and those who heard the speeches and songs that accompanied the pole's raising. It is possible, however, to distinguish crests, and in the old days an Indian stranger entering a village could find a particular clan by its totem crest.

Each figure depicted had a distinct mark. More than 100 symbols were used, those most often carved being the halibut, frog, beaver, bear, killer whale, seal, thunderbird, eagle and hawk. Parts of figures, such as a fin or fluted fish tail, or a wing of a bird were used. Wings meant the ability to fly; an ear meant special hearing power and understanding, and an eye meant having the power of life or the ability to change form.

Anthropologists recognize six different types of totem poles. Usually the largest, the potlatch pole commemorates a specific festival of feasting and gift-giving. House poles supported the central rafters of community houses. Mortuary poles were built with a hollow carved in the back to

Photo by Sixten Johanson/Tongass Historical Society

Totem Carver

Courtesy of Tongass Historical Society

Kyan pole, Ketchikan

Courtesy of Tongass Historical Society

Sun-Raven totem pole, Pennock Island

hold the ashes of the deceased. Memorial poles were the equivalent of tombstones, sometimes raised in memory of a chief by his successor. Heraldic poles recited the history of a family. And the ridicule pole shamed a person of high standing for failing to fulfil some obligation.

The origins of totem poles aren't known, but they were standing at the time European explorers sailed into the country. It is surmised that the abundance of food in Southeastern Alaska provided winter leisure time to develop the art form.

Before traders brought metal and a rainbow of pigments, totem poles were worked with tools of wood, stone, bone, antler, beaver teeth, and shells. Blades were lashed to handles with sinew, rawhide and spruce roots. Principal paint colors were black from coal or charcoal, red from iron ore and blue shades from copper oxides. Finely ground natural pigments were mixed with binders such as salmon eggs. Brushes were often made from porcupine hair.

Totem poles were not of a religious nature but were more like a European coat of arms. They are tributes to Northwest Indian Art.

Photo by U.S. Forest Service

Photo by Harriet Hunt/Tongass Historical Society

Chief Johnson totem pole and house, 1904

KETCHIKAN

Kitschkhin, or Just Fish Creek

The Tlingit Indian name for Ketchikan Creek was recorded in 1881, phonetically, as "Kitschkhin." One translation of the word stretches into "spread wings of a prostrate eagle," because midstream rocks divide the rushing white water to suggest that image, or, viewed from the heights of Deer Mountain, the course of the creek resembled the outspread wings of an eagle. Another version says the real name was Kats'kan, or "land belonging to Kats," an early Tlingit chief. Still another says the Tlingit name meant "wedge" because, from the slopes of Deer Mountain, Pennock Island looked like a wedge in the Narrows.

American seafarers passing charted Revillagigedo Island, however, reportedly called the stream much simpler "Fish Creek," for the hordes of spawning pink salmon that choke the creek every summer.

Whatever the true name, early stories say that a white man called Snow was operating a salmon saltery there as early as 1883. Then in 1885, an Irishman named Mike Martin was sent by Portland, Oregon, cannery interests to scout the shoreline's economic potential. The creek and surrounding land were owned as a fishing ground and canoe landing beach by the Kyan Indian clan and a Flathead Indian known as Charles "Paper Nose" Dickinson. Martin is said to have purchased 160 acres, including the creek site and today's downtown waterfront property, from Paper Nose Charlie.

The old story does not say how a Flathead (Kwakiutl) Indian happened to be in charge of a Tlingit land sale or what price was paid for the properties. But Martin did indeed end up owning the land and Paper Nose Charlie did exist. Tongass Indian elders remember that as children they sat on his knee and wondered about his nose. Charlie was said to have gotten into a fight with a Wrangell Indian who bit his nose off. After that, Charlie fashioned noses from paper and stuck them onto his face.

After the Tlingit sale of the Ketchikan townsite, cannery interests built salmon processing facilities on the shoreline, and brought in workmen. Construction required sawmills, loggers and sawyers. A community sprouted, and this new cluster of commerce became a supply center for prospectors, who needed assayers and lawyers. Single men needed hotels and restaurants, families needed carpenters to build homes, needed utilities, and teachers, schools, doctors and dentists.

And by 1900 the growing town decided it was time to become a city.

Courtesy of Tongass Historical Society

Newtown and Downtown, 1901

The Founding Of Ketchikan

Old documents shed a little light on the founding of Ketchikan but create a few mysteries as well. Records exist listing the names and occupations of the 95 men who signed a petition in July 1900 asking that the little community on Tongass Narrows become a city. The population at that time was certified on the petition as 800 permanent, bona fide residents, but was that a true figure? Only 103 voted. Eighty-two were for it, eighteen against and three apparently couldn't make up their minds after they took ballot in hand.

Although documents covering the petition and election do not say so, incorporation as a city must have given the city-to-be taxing powers: the petition cites a need for schools, peace-keeping "in a mining camp town," street improvements and sanitation, as well as fire protection. The light vote may indicate displeasure with any move that would create taxes. It may reflect the fact that many if not most of Ketchikan's primarily male citizens were engaged in seasonal, out-of-town employment that July. Or perhaps the founding fathers stretched the population truth a bit.

Fishing was a foundation of early Ketchikan's economic base, and so was mining. July happens to be the month of huge salmon runs and cannery operations. July would also be midsummer when miners would be prospecting in the hills or working claims before winter set in.

In the petition, Ketchikan was described as a supply center for the large Ketchikan Mining District. Among the signers were thirty-five who listed occupations as miners or prospectors, and two were attorneys representing Ketchikan's three law offices (lawyers traditionally followed mining discoveries to settle boundary and claim disputes).

The petition for incorporation as a city stated that Ketchikan was part of "the great highway of commerce between the States and Alaska on the

Photo by Harriet Hunt/Tongass Historical Society

Dock Street, Ketchikan, 1903

Inland Passage," the only available anchorage on Tongass Narrows — and the home of the customs house, as well. "The largest cannery in Alaska" was included in the petitioners' boast of various industries and professions. However, there are no signers listed as fishermen in a town of salteries and canneries. The only mariner listing is for "Paul Haury, sailor." No

Courtesy of Tongass Historical Society

Mike Martin (right) and friends

mill workers are listed either, although there is one "Joseph Gatins, logger." There are, however, two doctors, two dentists, a pharmacist and a barber included among the petitioners.

There are no female names on the petition, and for good reason. There is a story that an earlier petition had been submitted to the U.S. District Court for the District of Alaska. But, because it included names of female residents, it was struck down. The new one had to be drawn up.

Voter qualification instructions from District Court Judge M. C. Brown were clear: voters must be male citizens (or intending to become citizens), 21 years of age or older, bona fide residents of Alaska for one year and of Ketchikan for six months, and "owners of substantial property interests."

Photo by Harriet Hunt/Tongass Historical Society

Hunt's Store, Front Street, 1901

That final requirement may have been the reason for such a scanty voter turnout. Could the "miners and prospectors" signing the petition have been the property-owning "grubstakers" of the men in the hills?

The first elected common council was composed of Mayor Mike Martin, the first man to make a permanent home in Ketchikan; councilmen John W. Stedman, who five years after incorporation would open his Stedman Hotel; R. Boyd Young, a merchant; Robert Allison, mine owner; Dr. M. M. Hopkins, after whom Hopkins Alley was named; Harry E. Inman, carpenter, and J. R. Heckman, remembered as the inventor of the floating fish trap as well as founder of Heckman Company.

The first school board elected included well known F. J. Hunt, whose descendants live in Ketchikan today; J. H. Garrett; canneryman J. R. Beegle; Tom Heckman, and Judge Harvey Stackpole.

Among the miners and prospectors who signed the petition for incorporation as a city, a few had brief claims to fame. John W. Harris was probably the discoverer of the Harris mine near Hollis. H. C. Bradford was the partner of Chippewa Indian Antone de Nomie who discovered the Palmer Cove copper and gold mine. James Nesbitt discovered the Lucky Jim. Signer Charles Guzman, Chile-born grocery manager for J. R. Heckman, bought the rich Valparaiso mine at Dolomi from a Prince of Wales Indian called Johnson, and his son, who discovered the prospect in 1898 while hunting.

A signer with a tragic history was F. M. Gervais, the heavy-drinking brother of George Gervais, a partner in the 1900 discovery of the Lucky Nell mine on Prince of Wales. In later years Fred vanished and was assumed to have died near the trail over Sun-in-Hat Creek near Kasaan. A skull believed to have been Fred's sat for many years on a stump beside a bridge crossing the creek. By 1967 it, too, vanished.

But the pioneer names survive on the petition, and so does the city they founded.

Ingenuity Equals Vegetables

If anyone asked, and few do, why the public float at the foot of the downtown wooden dock No. 1 is named "Ryus Float," most oldtimers would probably assume it was named for pharmacist Emmett Ryus, who for many years had a drugstore on the dock side of Front Street at that location. And it was, indeed, named for the Ryus family, but not for the drugstore.

Retired barber Joe Sadlier, nephew of Mrs. Emmett Ryus, knows that real story. Emmett's father, Floyd Ryus, arrived in Ketchikan about 1904 from Graham, Texas. With him was his father, a civil engineer. The two men were looking for Alaska's famed "opportunity."

Their scouting included uninhabited Duke Island, some 30 miles south of Ketchikan, where they noticed two sizeable, shallow lakes which could be gravity-drained. If they accomplished that, no land would have to be cleared. The lakes were drained, allowed to dry and tilled. On the lakebeds they planted produce and berries. The family also kept chickens and cows, and oldtimers at Metlakatla remember stories of going to Duke Island for milk.

The Ryuses devised rail tracks, built from two-by-fours from Metlakatla's sawmill, and fashioned cars to ride those tracks to tidewater. Produce was then freighted to Ketchikan and offloaded at what became known as Ryus Float, in the family's honor.

Long since abandoned, that old farm still produces bumper crops of raspberries, there for the picking — if you know how to find them. They are just beyond Floyd, Emmett, Ruth and Helen Islands, named for the farming Mr. Ryus and his three children.

The Questionable Virtue of Creek Street

Prostitution was as much a part of Ketchikan's history as it was of the Old West's, or any frontier society. But as wives and children, school teachers and missionaries settled in the new city of Ketchikan at the beginning of the 20th century, it became obvious to the very first elected city council that something had to be done about The Girls.

The city fathers did not outlaw the selling of female favors but did decide, in 1903, to require the sporting women to move from their various locations around the new city to a relatively secluded part of town — Creek Street. This move may have been prompted by council member Dr. Hopkins, who discovered (to his dismay) two houses of ill repute operating within yards of his own respectable office and home. Out of sight, out of mind.

Creek Street was and is a plank boardwalk edging Ketchikan Creek at the base of Boston Smith hill. In 1903 the abutted false front buildings of Stedman Street probably partially screened the double rows of bawdy houses perched on piling or balanced on ledges of rock along the creek's bank. Some were probably homes when the "rezoning" came in 1903; others may already have been "houses."

Creek Street structures began in the early days with No. 1, across the creek falls at the end of a now-vanished upland footbridge extending from a warren of rakishly angled, racial minority dwellings and buildings housing such businesses as shooting galleries, cafes and a Chinese laundry that spread along the creek bank to the home of Tlingit Chief Johnson. The totem pole that marked his house was raised in 1902 and a replica still stands in its original location. The other end of Creek Street's half-circle boardwalk merged at the creek's mouth with the main thoroughfare Stedman Street in the heart of what was the old town, or "Indian town."

A decade after the city edict formally established Ketchikan's red-light district, a 1914 fire insurance map shows a shingle mill, shed and log platform along the creek among the twelve houses of ill repute and one private home lining the upland side of the boardwalk. On the Stedman Street side of the creek, two more houses of ill repute brazenly shared a block of Indian town's main thoroughfare with a boat shed, mission church, hand laundry, general mercantile, a restaurant and saloon.

Houses of prostitution were identified on the fire map by the symbol "F. B." for "Female Boarders," a euphemism for prostitutes. The shingle mill's flume, which carried water through the woods along the creek's course from the falls farther upstream, may have marked the later "Married Men's Trail," used by those who wished to visit the Creek without being seen.

Ketchikan had only two levels of government in the days before 1959's Statehood. One was the city, which dealt with the matters of zoning, utilities and fire protection, schools, streets, sanitation and minor law enforcement. The other was the Territorial government whose federal law enforcement responsibility was under the jurisdiction of U. S. marshals. Under Territorial law, a house of prostitution was defined as a house having more than two female boarders. Therefore, most of the Creek Street brothels had, at least officially, only two female occupants.

An exception was No. 5 Creek Street, The Star, which was at the turn of the century just a small dwelling. A large dance hall addition with upstairs

Photo by Case & Draper/Tongass Historical Society

Cooper shop, barrel factory on Creek Street, 1905

rooms was added sometime before 1914. A 1917 property deed describes it as a two-story, twelve-room frame dwelling. The original part of the structure is clearly labeled "F. B." on the 1914 fire map, but the attached dance hall with upstairs rooms is not. It is possible that its status as a dance hall with a need for dancing partners excluded it from bawdy house designation.

Creek Street was a lively place. The Girls called themselves sporting women, not whores. Their houses were party centers, not the tiny one-room one-cot cribs of Juneau or Fairbanks. Their parties were popular. Ketchikan was the first port of call for the fishing fleets headed north and the final port of call for those same fishermen heading south with pockets full of money. A crew of a halibut boat might number as many as fifteen men. Salmon seiner crews might number as many as eight. And Ketchikan's docks were crowded with fishing boats.

Creek Street was noisy and noisome as well when the tide was out and the creek level too low to handle the sanitation problem — facilities emptied directly into the creek. There were fights over Girls, and fights between Girls, suicide threats and attempts, and brawls. The Girls were at one time required to put wire mesh screens over their windows to prevent drunken revelers from putting their fists through the glass.

An occasional body would be found floating near the mouth of the creek at dawn. While minor infractions of the peace were handled by city police, a fatal knifing or a case involving a "floater" were cases for federal marshals. But federal lawmen were spread thin over the vast expanse of Territorial Alaska.

In efforts to alleviate the too-obvious problems of Creek Street, the city tried legal regulation and control of the illegal industry. And "industry" it was.

Fleets of fishing boats called at Ketchikan partly because of the promises of the Creek and to spend money citywide for repairs and stores, to cash checks, to lay in illegal supplies of liquor during Prohibition as well as to visit the houses of ill fame. Most of the Girls were big spenders themselves. They bought the best — clothes, furs, jewelry, shoes, cosmetics, appliances, groceries, housewares, and steamship tickets as well as paying for utilities, fuel, house repairs and remodeling projects. And they paid cash.

When the Creek became too rowdy and confident of its economic importance, city police launched raids and collected tribute money. When pressure from reform groups, churches and mothers' groups became insistent, new rules and regulations were put into effect. At one time the Girls could not venture into the respectable parts of town at all. At other times they couldn't go beyond Bawden Street. There was one period when they could go into town only on Wednesdays. But desk clerks at downtown hotels admitted that when a drummer was in town, they would allow the Girls to slip up to the salesman's room.

This street of sin did not go unnoticed by the outside world. Tourists were part of Alaska's summer scene from the earliest days and, during their Ketchikan stops, included Creek Street on their itineraries as they do today. They did not stroll the boardwalk then, but they craned their necks to see the Girls waving merrily from their porches, drying their hair in the sun or hanging their laundry on porch clotheslines. Travel

Photo by William Lattin/Tongass Historical Society

Creek Street, 1930's

writers, crusaders, missionaries and some of Alaska's early aspiring politicians all penned or printed their outraged comments about Ketchikan's red-light district.

Occasionally such pressure on the city's image resulted in temporary closures of the Creek, at which times the Girls left for vacations or quietly moved into other locations until the furor cooled. The street was empty and quiet during its extended closure during World War II, but opened once again before federal and local reform pressure forced its final closure in 1954.

The rooting out of this lucrative "industry" was not without incident. A police chief and his captain were convicted of financial interests in the business. Lawsuits and libel trials followed the oral and printed accusations of both sides of the issue. There were firings and whisper campaigns against public servants, a suicide and at least one other death under mysterious circumstances. There are a few people left who are still angry about those troubled days.

The younger Girls scattered to locations more welcoming. A few of the older sporting women chose to remain in Ketchikan, living in their old properties on their savings. Annie Watkins of No. 4 Creek Street, who was rumored to have a little black book of local names, died in 1966 — the fate of her black book unknown. Thelma Baker died in a fire in the Star at No. 5 in 1972. Dolly Arthur of No. 24, the last of the well known Girls, died in 1975.

For half a century Ketchikan's red-light district frolicked and rollicked. And then, when the time was right, it was closed for good and became just another memory of a frontier past.

Courtesy of Ketchikan Daily News

Dolly's house, interior

A Moonshine Tale

This ditty was written in 1898 when the U. S. Customs House was on Mary Island south of Ketchikan. Alaska was governed by the U. S. Army and as such, prohibition of liquor was in effect. According to the song, "the boys" managed to get a shipment of good Canadian liquor — not moonshine — past customs, and composed this song as they waited in Whiskey Cove on Pennock Island — across from downtown Ketchikan — to smuggle it into town on the tide.

"On Tongass Narrows"
[As sung by the Ketchikan Glee Club, 1898]

As I sit near the camp fire in the cabin,
My reflections are unpleasant as can be.
I am thinking of a girl back in Seattle
Who is waiting there and wishing to see me.
And she hopes some day I'll make a winner,
But I know she is not the kind to pray.
She will jolly up the gang, the little sinner,
While I knock about Alaska, far away.

[Chorus]

For it's raining to beat Hell on Tongass Narrows,
But at Ketchikan the boys tonight are gay,
For the Customs House was slack at Mary Island
And we got good booze from just across the way.

Courtesy of Tongass Historical Society

"In Defiance of the Dry Squad, Traitor's Cove near Loring, Alaska. July, 1924."

Photo by Bertha Wells/Tongass Historical Society

Newtown miners, 1900

Courtesy of Tongass Historical Society

Tree Point Lighthouse, 1920's

Photo by Jackie James

Metlakatla dancers

Photo by Hall Anderson

Raising Beaver-Eagle totem pole, Saxman, May 1986

Photo by Hall Anderson

Hydaburg totem poles

Photo by Hall Anderson

Abandoned fish traps, Prince of Wales Island

Photo by Chip Porter

Alaska power trollers fishing for king salmon, Whale Bay

Photo by Chip Porter

Thomas Basin, Jens Jensen's *Swiftsure* in foreground

Photo by Hall Anderson

Alaska Marine Highway ferry, M/V *Matanuska*, drydock maintenance, 1989

Photo by Chip Porter

Seining for pink salmon, Revillagigedo Passage

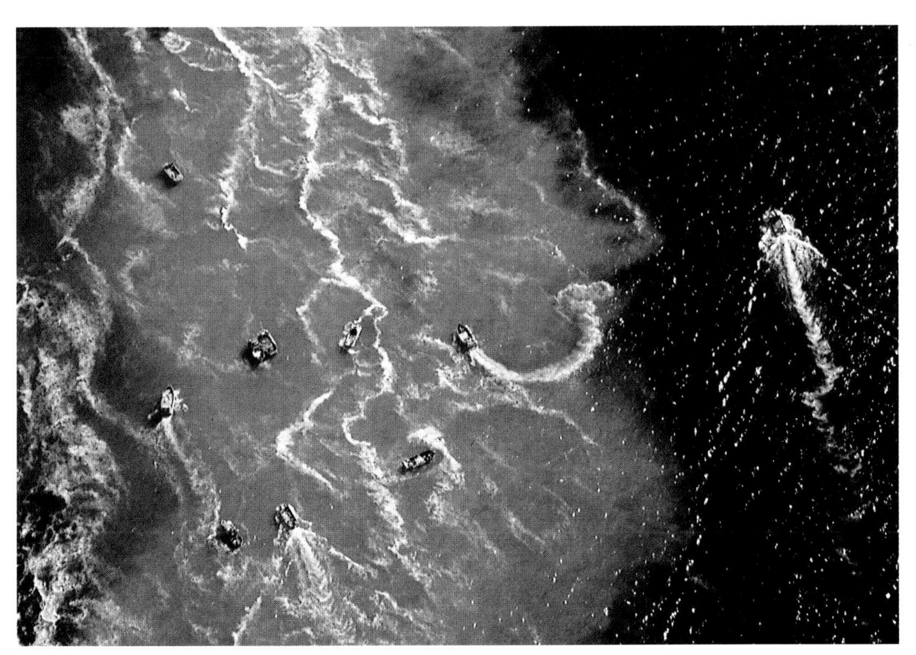

Photo by Chip Porter

Herring roe gillnet fishery, Kah Shakes, 1989

Photo by Chip Porter

Happy Eager lumber ship, Dora Bay, Prince of Wales Island

Photo by Don "Bucky" Dawson

Family moves by Goose, Smith Cove Logging Camp, 1983

Photo by Hall Anderson

Labouchere Bay Logging Camp, Prince of Wales Island

Photo by Steve Shrum

Ketchikan Pulp Company, 1991

Photo by Steve Shrum

Strolling in City Park near Fair Building, 1950's

Photo by Hall Anderson

Fourth of July parade, Ketchikan, 1990

Photo by Hall Anderson

City Float and Water Street at night, 1992

Photo by Don "Bucky" Dawson

Ketchikan's annual production of "Fish Pirate's Daughter," 1986

Photo by Steve Shrum

Black bear with salmon, 1991

Photo by Chip Porter

Duck hunters, Andy Taylor and Dave Doyon, 1989

Photo by Steve Shrum

"Fly"-fishing in Misty Fiords, 1991

Photo by U.S. Forest Service

El Capitan caves

Photo by Steve Shrum

Little Goat Lake, Misty Fiords, 1991

Photo by Don "Bucky" Dawson

Twin Otter alongside the face of Punchbowl Mountain, Misty Fiords, 1992

MINING

A Golden History

Gold fever! Ketchikan was not immune to this malady as steamships jam-packed with feverish would-be miners stopped en route to the Klondike gold fields during the Gold Rush of '98. No doubt some local prospectors joined their fellows for the trip north. But there was hope for riches from the earth right here on Ketchikan's own island and even greater hopes for rich prospects on Prince of Wales Island to the west.

Gold was the dream, but copper, too, might mean riches when world markets were right. The oldest mining claim in the southern Southeast Alaska region, probably the first lode location in all of Alaska, was the Copper Queen on Kasaan Bay on the east coast of Prince of Wales. It was discovered in 1867 by Charles Vincent Baronovich, who worked it for a time. A Yugoslav by birth, he was a veteran of the 1849 Gold Rush to California and later prospected the Cariboo country of British Columbia before trying his luck in Alaska.

The Copper Queen was reactivated in 1900 and was worked until 1902. There was extensive development for the era — surface cuts, a shaft near the beach, a road to the tidewater shipping point and main workings at a creek's fork at 300 feet.

Kasaan Peninsula stretches down from the east coast of the island with its snout in Clarence Strait due west of Ketchikan's north end residential district. It was, and is, rich with copper prospects. At the head of the peninsula's bay was The Joker mine, a 1906 copper discovery which in 1919 was developed for its platinum and by 1925 had seventy men on the payroll. But it closed in 1926 when platinum prices sagged.

Copper and platinum were not the only metals waiting to be discovered on Prince of Wales Island. The mountains backdropping Kasaan Bay and dividing the island east from west were, and are, rich with gold. There are success stories recorded and dismal failures.

The entire history of mining activity in the Ketchikan District — as elsewhere — was marked by natural or economic disasters: lack of capital, discoveries too far from salt water, interruptions by national economic depressions, global wars and just plain bad luck. Slides would bury a year's work. Backers would pull out. Partners would quarrel and separate, with losses to both. And some miners just disappeared, whether accidentally or intentionally. Obituaries of the day report a disproportionate number of suicides among miners.

But there was the odd story of wealth gleaned from the earth, the miner's dream. A carpenter from Washington state, out hunting west of Hollis at the head of Kasaan Bay, stumbled across a rich gold discovery in 1900. He named it the Puyallup Mine after his hometown. He reportedly knew nothing about mining and sold the claim. But men named Bill Baker and Robert Allison reportedly took in $200,000 in the first years of the mine's operation.

Lucky Mike McGilvery discovered the Blackbird gold mine behind Hollis in 1900. He apparently never said much about his discovery, but rumors persisted that he brought gold with him every time he traveled to Ketchikan. The stories died with him in 1915.

More stories probably paralleled the tale of Billy Metzdorf, remembered because he struck it rich, went south with a pocketful of money to get married but returned shortly after — broke, and alone.

Photo by Harriet Hunt/Tongass Historical Society

Hadley, 1904

Courtesy of Tongass Historical Society

Shafthouse and Tramway, Sealevel

Photo by Harriet Hunt/Tongass Historical Society

Golden Fleece Mine, Dolomi, 1906

A Lost Gold Mine

There is a story of a lost gold mine, located near Tree Point on the mainland just south of Duke Island. The story goes that when Ketchikan was nothing more than a trading post back in the late 1880s, a stranger arrived in town with a large quantity of rich gold quartz. He sold it to a trader for a "handsome sum," went on a spree, and then bought supplies and loaded them in his boat.

The stranger slipped away even though the men of the town dogged his heels, hoping for a hint about the location of his mine. He was never seen in Ketchikan again.

Years later a keeper at Tree Point lighthouse stumbled across an abandoned cabin while hunting far back in the hills. In the cabin were quartz samples and rusty mining tools. He, too, had heard the story and was sure he'd found the lost lode. He returned to the lighthouse, but he was never able to locate the cabin again. A later light keeper also stumbled across the cabin and he, too, was never able to find it again.

But there are those who swear it is there, waiting for the lucky discoverer.

Photo by Schallerer/Tongass Historical Society

Marble quarry, View Cove

An Island of Marble

The word "mining," when speaking of Alaska, is almost always associated with "gold." But Alaska was, and is, a storehouse of almost every mineral mankind ever utilized. One of them is marble. Early settlers of Wrangell and Ketchikan made limited local use of marble deposits in their vicinities, primarily for gravestones. There are stories of logging roads, paved with low grade crushed marble, seen as white lines from the air.

But at the turn of the century, gold prospectors clambering through the coastal wilds of northwest Prince of Wales Island found something they weren't looking for — magnificent, high quality marble deposits. Letters reached the Vermont Marble Company in New England, telling of "mountains of marble, quantity beyond calculation and quality to which no other marble in the world was superior." And, it was true. There are vast marble deposits, even an entire island of marble.

Small independent companies began operation in the field. A decade later, in 1909, Vermont Marble began large-scale quarry work on Marble Island, working the pale-colored deposits estimated to be five to six miles long and two to three miles wide. Deposits of darker hues, prized for trim, were found. By 1914 there were seventy to 110 men at work.

From several remote locations on the west coast of an Alaska island most people had never heard of came the marble for elegant buildings from coast to coast. Work was halted by World War I, and postwar construction tastes ran to concrete rather than marble. Operations never resumed, except when one quarry was briefly reopened in 1926 for a specific purpose — to quarry marble for the Washington state capitol.

The old, classical architectural styles featuring marble have been replaced by the practical modern. But public buildings from coast to coast, built with Alaska's marble, still stand.

One is Alaska's own capitol building. Another is the Pearl Harbor Naval Hospital in Honolulu. In Minnesota, St.Paul's Great Northern Railway Building features Alaska marble; in Pennsylvania, Pittsburgh's Finance Building; in Massachusetts, Boston's Orpheum Theater, and in Victoria, B. C., the Sayward Building.

In Seattle, Alaska marble stands proud in the Arctic Club, Hoge Building, L. C. Smith and Bank of California Buildings, the McCormick Hotel and the Courthouse. Tacoma's National Realty Building, Perkins Building and Tacoma Building are adorned with Alaska marble. So is the U. S. Post Office in Bellingham and Walla Walla County Courthouse.

In Portland, Oregon, see the Spaulding, Wilcox, Oregon Journal and Multnomah Buildings.

California's Los Angeles tributes to Alaska marble are the Black Building, the Los Angeles Investment Building, the Inglewood Community Mausoleum, Merchants National Bank Building and the Southern Pacific Passenger Station.

Also see San Francisco's Flatiron Building, Hobart Building and Odd Fellows Building. San Diego's Central Mortgage Building and U. S. Post Office are tributes to Alaska marble, as is Sacramento's Capital National Bank Building and Forum Building.

Alaska marble also was shipped inland to grace Boise, Idaho's, State Capitol and Gem Building, and the U. S. Post Offices in Moscow and Lewiston, Idaho.

The Ford Commercial Building in Great Falls, Montana, is adorned with Alaska marble as are Utah's Walker Building, National City Bank Building, Empress Theater and Newhouse Hotel in Salt Lake City and the Eccles Building in Ogden.

Alaska's marble quarries are abandoned and silent now, except for the occasional ring of a geologist's pick hammer testing samples of the beautiful "baked" limestone rock that may once again come into architectural fashion.

Courtesy of Tongass Historical Society

Marble Island, Tokeen, 1915

Photo by Fisher Studio/Tongass Historical Society

Canning line, 1930's

Photo by Schallerer/Tongass Historical Society

Can reforming line

FISHING

'The Canned Salmon Capital of the World!'

In 1883 a Mr. Snow started a fish saltery near the mouth of Ketchikan Creek, apparently with the consent of the Tlingit Indians who had a traditional summer fish camp there. His saltery appears to have been short-lived. By 1885 there were three small canneries nearby and all were reported to be losing money.

But in 1887, one cannery (built where Downtown Drugstore is today) packed 5,000 cases. By 1889 its pack had increased to 13,000 cases. In 1890 a new saltery went into business, using four seine nets and employing 50 men; the first year the catch was 20,000 red salmon, 40,000 cohos and 500,000 pink salmon. What couldn't be salted was sold to the cannery.

In 1903 trolling for king salmon began on a small scale, mostly by lone fishermen in dories powered by oars or sails. This fishery increased rapidly when gas boats were introduced and cold storage facilities became available. As the fishing industry grew, the need for cold storage facilities had become obvious.

Oldtimers remember that before there were cold storages, fishermen picked up large chunks of icebergs which had come from the LeConte glacier near Petersburg — Mother Nature's own vast icebox. The men put the ice in a dory and after taking it aboard the fishing boat, pounded it into small pieces with sturdy sticks made for that purpose. Then it was thrown into the hold of the boat to be used for icing fish — dense glacier ice melts slowly.

In 1906 a group of Ketchikan businessmen, headed by John Stedman, (who later built the elegant Stedman Hotel on the site of the first downtown cannery) interested the New England Fish Company of Boston in building the first cold storage plant here. Work was begun in 1907 and completed in 1908.

The canning industry in Ketchikan had been given little attention until a rise in canned salmon prices in 1910 prompted others to invest in the industry. In 1911 and 1912 several new cannery ventures were begun, among them the Ward Cove cannery. Another was the Pure Food Company located on the water side of what today is the corner of Front and Mill Streets; fish from the first privately owned fish trap was delivered to Pure Foods.

By 1913, New England's cold storage success stimulated another local group to build the larger Ketchikan Cold Storage (KCS), located at the

Photo by Jane Gelormino/Tongass Historical Society

Sliming crew at cold storage

waterfront site of today's downtown Berth II Eagle Park. KCS had a capacity of freezing seventy tons of ice and 90,000 pounds of fish per day, with storage space for 7,500,000 pounds. This cold storage capacity attracted the halibut industry, which began to grow in importance.

By 1920, Ketchikan's fishery industry was becoming of major importance. In one day in late June of that year, thirty-seven trollers unloaded salmon and halibut to the tune of $5,657.96. The largest catch earned $816.55 and the smallest — a boy fisherman — earned $2.31. In today's dollars that would amount to well over $16,000 for the highliner and about $42 for the boy.

By 1930, more than 150 halibut boats called at Ketchikan and more than 1,000 salmon boats supplied the 13 canneries and cold storages. The value of the canned salmon pack in the district was $5 million; fresh salmon, mild cured salmon, halibut and other fish products were valued at many thousands of dollars more.

Courtesy of Tongass Historical Museum

Sharp freezer, New England Cold Storage, 1920

It is curious that, until Silver Lining Seafoods opened its retail line in 1986, there had been only two previous fish markets in Ketchikan. In the 1930s Marco and then Angelo Bussanich had a fish market near where the tunnel is located today. The market offered not only salmon, halibut, cod and red snapper, but delicacies such as octopus and squid as well. It closed when Angelo Bussanich retired in the 1940s.

In the mid-1940s, Lyle Wallace and Lambert Ratcliffe briefly operated a retail fresh fish market on Dock Street.

Possibly fish markets met with little success in the early days because Ketchikan was the salmon capital of the world! — and everyone either had their own supply of fish or a friend who did. That's largely true even now.

Today the diversified fisheries remain an important base of Ketchikan's economy.

A China House Tale

Today fish cannery lines are manned by local youth, by summer-vacation college students from around the nation and by itinerant workers from across the continent. This was not always so. In the early days the stateside-based cannery interests brought in their own workers. The first were Chinese, hired en masse from a "hiring boss" and brought to Southeastern Alaska in the holds of sailing ships.

The late Ralph A. Bartholomew, pioneer Ketchikan businessman, remembered the "China Houses" that were part of the cannery scene in the days when Chinese laborers were used to slime and clean fish. Each cannery provided a large bunkhouse, or "China House," and paid the workers $100 each for the summer salmon season.

One or two Chinese were sent ahead of the others early each season to plant a garden near the bunkhouse to provide the crews' own Oriental vegetables. The Chinese crews brought along their own pigs and chickens, bags of rice, pottery bowls and their round, slim-necked pottery bottles of rice wine. During the fish canning season itself, the Chinese were given all the scrap fish that came in on the scows. With shelter provided, they fed themselves until mid-September when they were paid and freighted south again.

By the 1920s the influx of Chinese workers was looked upon with suspicion by many Americans nationwide as a Yellow Peril. The China hiring bosses were also demanding better conditions. The cannery owners tried several other minority groups and finally replaced the Chinese with Filipino labor, the Philippine Islands at the time being a possession of the United States.

In the 1960s Ketchikan's municipal laws were recodified. Deleted from the code were old ordinances dealing with the smoking of opium, with drunkenness and rowdiness on Chinese holidays, with pigs and chickens allowed to escape onto city streets. In Bayview Cemetery records, there are a few Chinese listed as buried there in the early years. The names are listed twice, by the first of their double Chinese names and again by the last name, not knowing which was the proper order.

Today's itinerant cannery workers spend the brief canning season in tents, in variously adapted campers and in quarters on a cannery-provided barge.

Photo by Sixten Johanson/Tongass Historical Society

Brailing floating trap, Bond Bay, 1946

The Controversial Fish Trap

The use of fish traps to harvest salmon was a controversial issue in Alaska almost from the day the first commercial trap was installed. Fishermen resented the canneries' mechanical competition; traps were blamed for the decline of salmon stocks in mid-century. The new State of Alaska abolished traps immediately after Statehood in 1959. (Only four remain within the boundaries of the state, those at the federal Indian Reserve at Metlakatla, Alaska's only Indian reservation.)

The Native traps were usually rock or pole barricades that penned in fish that had moved in at high tide and were thus trapped when the tide went out. The first modern copies were also stationary, nets attached to piling driven near shore. They were located strategically to catch the largest runs of fish possible. The possibilities of such bountiful supplies of fish caught with minimal human labor sparked the interest and ingenuity of

Photo by Sixten Johanson/Tongass Historical Society

Pile trap, McLean Arm, 1934

businessmen who were, at the turn of the century, building salmon canneries up and down Alaska's coastline.

J. R. Heckman, pioneer canneryman and a member of Ketchikan's first common council, is credited with inventing the first floating fish trap about 1910. Floating traps were made of frameworks of logs, usually large hemlock, to which wire net was attached. The traps could be towed each season to known deepwater locations of heavy runs of salmon. There they were secured with huge trap anchors. A net pouch hung down to a necessary depth with a large opening which milling fish would enter, and attempting to continue with the tide, would seek out a smaller opening which led into spillers where they were trapped, but not killed. Cannery boats tended the traps on schedules, webbing up and brailing the fish into the holds of the cannery boats.

The efficiency of the traps was also their eventual undoing. It was true that trap operations insured freshly caught, prime fish — the fish went directly from the trap to the cannery without delay; those caught by traditional fishing methods stayed aboard the small boats through the fishing periods and during runs to the cannery. But the traps also contributed to the depletion of the resource.

Fishermen for years had complained that certain streams proximate to fish traps, once rich with salmon, no longer had fish runs. Fishermen felt they were losing their livelihoods to the traps. But Territorial Alaska's fisheries were governed by sometimes disinterested, often heavily lobbied federal agencies thousands of miles away in Washington, D. C.

The cannery interests had the ear of Washington: the cannery business was lucrative, it created shore employment and business for banks, for suppliers and service businesses; it needed logs and wire rope for traps, lumber for cannery expansion and fish boxes. Canned fish was a main cargo item of the steamer freight business, ships which also provided the remote islands of Southeastern Alaska with passenger service. The cannery statistics about employment carried more weight at that time than the fishermen's concern about depletion of the stocks of fish and their resulting loss of employment.

Then in the mid-1930s, when the word "Depression" was synonymous with "unemployment" nationwide, Congress was finally willing to record the statements of fishermen and the anti-trap arguments of Alaska's delegate to Congress. The fishermen related specific stories of the declining salmon resource; then-delegate Dan A. Sutherland of Juneau outlined the history of traps and the fact that such devices had been abolished everywhere in the world — except Alaska.

However, the focus of this Congressional hearing held in 1936 was employment, not fish traps. Much of Alaska's economy and employment was dependent on the canneries, and thus on the traps. It was the industry whose taxes fed the federal treasury and alleviated the federal fiscal responsibility to the Territory. The findings of that 1936 U. S. House Committee on Merchant Marine and Fisheries hearing are not included in the text of the meetings.

But it was not until Statehood in 1959 that the new state abolished fish traps and the management of the state's fishery resources was in the hands of the state. The salmon resource slowly reestablished itself. Today the threat to North Pacific salmon stocks is illegal drift net fishing by Asian Pacific Rim countries. Alaska's Congressional delegates continue to fight the threat.

Fish Pirates!

The phrase "fish pirate" today generally refers to Taiwanese, Korean and possibly Japanese fishermen who allegedly are in the warmer waters of the mid-Pacific to fish squid, but who slip northward into the colder waters of the North Pacific and illegally net, or pirate, Alaska's feeding salmon resource. It is a serious charge.

In Ketchikan's early days, however, a fish pirate was something of a hero to his fellow fishermen and a scoundrel only to the cannery interests. Fish pirating was a way of life, involving outright theft, threats of bodily harm and a great deal of dishonesty. But if a fish pirate was caught and charged, sympathetic juries of his peers would let him off.

In those days, there were hundreds of fish traps up and down the coastlines of Alaska, owned by canneries, or by individuals with their catches contracted to canneries. The mechanical floating traps were able to cage a great number of fish at one time, fish still alive and unharmed until they were loaded into a cannery tender and hurried back to the home plant for processing. Such fish brought higher prices than fish caught by traditional boat-fishing methods in which fish would be in a boat's hold for varying lengths of time before being brought to canneries for sale.

Fishermen considered the traps threatening to their livelihoods. Especially in poor seasons, any method to gain those trap fish for themselves was considered fair game.

Each trap had a round-the-clock watchman hired by the cannery. His duties included discouraging theft and protecting cannery interests. But sometimes, if he were handed a hundred dollars or so, he would turn his back or disappear into the trap shack and allow the fish pirates to brail fish out of the trap. The fish pirates then sped back to the cannery and sold their purloined fish, sometimes to the same cannery from which they had been stolen.

Traps were not allowed to operate on Sundays, but sometimes trap watchmen would allow the trap to fish on that day of rest and then, with a clear conscience, sell the catch to fish pirates.

The incidence of pirating became so bad that the canneries hired patrol boats to watch their watchmen. Then they hired Pinkerton men (professional detectives) to man the trap shacks.

The fish pirates responded with even cleverer methods to steal. Cannery tenders often towed fish scows of trap fish behind when salmon runs were heavy. The scows often held as much as twice the amount of the tender.

There is a story of just such a situation: The tender and a following scow were returning to the cannery with full loads in both when they ran into fog and darkness. They continued slowly on their way to the cannery, but when the fog lifted, the crew saw that they were towing a log raft! The crafty fish pirates scored again.

Sometimes the fish pirates would throw wet burlap bags over the names of their boats so they couldn't be recognized by the trap watchman. There were a few shootings, but no one remembers any injuries on either side. It was just the way it was.

There is another story of a pair of college boys from Washington state who operated a seine boat that didn't even have a seine! They simply pirated fish and paid their way through college. The canneries even chartered a boat to follow this elusive seiner but never caught it. The story expands with one of the pair who is said to have bought canneries himself and sold out to become a millionaire.

Eventually, the pirating of fish became a federal offense, which slowed the theft somewhat. It would have meant FBI men on the case.

The problem was solved altogether in 1959 when the Legislature of the brand new state outlawed fish traps. By that time the salmon resource had declined to serious levels. In the 30-plus years since that time, the salmon resource has gradually recovered. Whether that fact reflects Nature's own capricious cycles or whether it was due to the banning of the traps is still debated...occasionally.

A Century of Halibut Fishing

Archeological studies indicate that Pacific halibut was an important food fish to the Indian tribes of the Pacific Northwest and Alaska, and part of their culture and lore, long before European explorers discovered the tasty creature. The huge halibut's firm, white, boneless, mild-flavored flesh was a gourmet's delight, but it was believed in the last century that there was no way to ship the unprocessed fish from its Pacific Coast habitat to markets distant from Puget Sound ports.

Then in 1888 a 79-foot sailing vessel, the *Oscar and Hattie,* after rounding Cape Horn, arrived in Seattle too late for pelagic (high seas)

Photo by Fisher Studio/Tongass Historical Society

Halibut schooners, Ketchikan

sealing and decided to try for halibut. Fishing was good, and in that year a 50,000-pound shipment of iced halibut left by rail for lucrative East Coast markets. The rush was on, and for two years sailing ships dominated the fishery.

Then they were crowded out by company-owned steamers, able to travel farther from port, and manned by crews of up to 35 men. Halibut fishing by the steamers was conducted from small dories carried aboard the ships. Each sail-powered dory was manned by two fishermen who could fish many hooks in one day. But the steamer fleet was so efficient, reaching a peak in 1914, that catches began to decline, making the fishery increasingly unprofitable for the large ships.

One by one they were replaced by a fleet of independently owned vessels, and the schooner became the dominant vessel fishing halibut. The fishery began to move north. Halibut schooners began to homeport in Ketchikan in the 1920s and by the early 1930s, it was home port to a fleet of more than 150 halibut boats. And each year in April, into the 1960s, the Norwegian community in Ketchikan welcomed the arriving northbound

Seattle-based halibut fleet with ceremony. Ketchikan became the nerve-center of the North Pacific halibut fleet.

Ketchikan's resident halibut fishermen, mainly Norwegian, built homes on what became known as Captains' Hill, a neighborhood of homes around upper Water Street. In 1930 the First Lutheran Church was built on a rock outcropping near the water. It is a landmark and a reference point for the old Norwegian neighborhood.

Some of the principal fish buyers in those heyday years were at nearby Prince Rupert, B. C., which has rail connections to the East Coast. Marine outfitters were established along Ketchikan's waterfront, supplying groceries and gear; they managed the boats' accounts, cashed checks, paid bills and figured the balance, and served as post offices for fisherman mail.

The first schooners operated on gasoline engines but switched to diesel when that became economical. At first schooners used dories for the catch. But it was dangerous work, particularly in the winter, and as a result the schooners converted to setlining, or longlining, in which the gear is set

Courtesy of Tongass Historical Society

Schooner *Eagle* taking ice at NEFCO

and hauled from the schooner itself. Stern chutes were designed for setting gear and power gurdies installed to retrieve the setlines.

Longliners make sets of long, buoy-suspended lines anchored at each end and suspended by buoys with flags. Ground lines, to which hooks are attached, are laid along the ocean floor. The ground line, with the hooked fish, is later reeled in.

Almost all schooners were built prior to the 1930s and many are still fishing today. While schooners were very efficient at halibut fishing, they were not easily used in other fisheries such as seining for salmon or herring, or pot fishing for crab. The lack of versatility created a need for a vessel design which could be used in any number of fisheries.

This led to the development of the "combination" vessel. Today's halibut fisherman can participate in more than one fishery — seining or trolling for salmon, pot fishing for crab, trawling for flounders and roundfish, longlining for tuna or even chartering the boat for sport fishing.

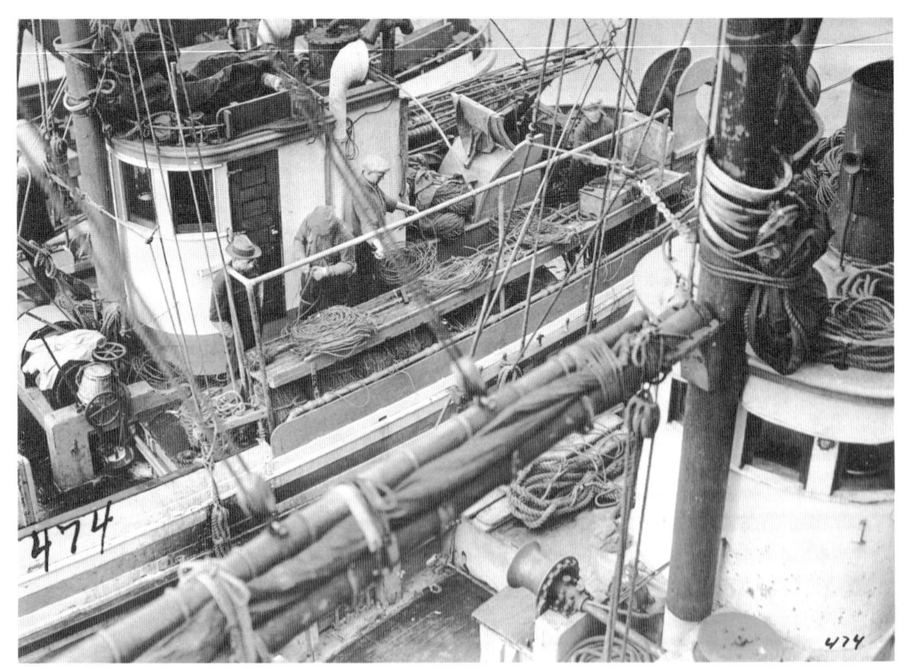

Photo by Fisher Studio/Tongass Historical Society

Halibut schooner crew overhauling gear

Courtesy of Tongass Historical Society

Niagara on herring set, 1914

The days of the schooners are gone, although a few old schooners still fish and call at Ketchikan on occasion, as do the newer vessels passing through. Kodiak and Dutch Harbor replaced Ketchikan as the halibut capital of Alaska. Ketchikan's Fish Exchange shack on the downtown dock, where buyers bid both for salmon and halibut, is also gone. But there's still that smell of fish and tides each spring, a feast or two of fresh halibut and all the memories of days gone by.

(Information provided by former Mayor and Ketchikan Cold Storage manager James G. Pinkerton, from material supplied by the International Pacific Halibut Commission.)

Photo by Fisher Studio/Tongass Historical Society

Ketchikan Cold Storage, 1930

Baked Halibut

From 1955 until 1974, it was the rare youngster in Ketchikan who missed school on Friday. That was because Friday was the day Karen Sund, school cook, baked halibut for her charges. Mrs. Sund, originally from Norway, has never kept her simple recipe a secret, and now many of her former students, their parents and grandparents enjoy her baked halibut, which is especially tasty when the big fish is brought home from the salt waters near Ketchikan.

This Is "The Recipe":

Cut halibut slices into three- or four-inch squares. Dip all sides in melted butter and then in fine bread crumbs. Place close together in a baking dish and bake at 400 degrees for 17 to 20 minutes, depending on the thickness of the squares. So simple, and so unfailingly good.

The secret of all good fish dishes is not to overcook. The crumb coating on the halibut does not have to be a deep brown, just a nice golden color.

Enjoy!

TIMBER

Timber-r-r: 1900 to 1950
In the Beginning...

Natives of the North Pacific coast were using local wood for domestic goods, canoes, buildings and totem poles long before 1778, when Captain Cook landed his ship near Nootka Sound to repair its rotted, storm-damaged masts with the tall coastal timber.

Within ten years of Cook's landing, Russian fur traders were settling Alaska's coastline. These colonists cut timber mainly for local use, and began to export incidentally as their ships began taking on logs to stabilize the lightweight fur cargos. Later, the Russians packed ice in sawdust from their mills to ship to San Francisco during the California Gold Rush of '49.

Before the turn of the century, Alaskans could harvest timber for personal use legally from mining claims under the term "innocent trespass." Federal officials might stretch the interpretation of the law so small businesses too could take modest amounts of timber for a small fee. However, federal rules designed to encourage logging often complicated it, making logging in early Alaska difficult. In 1902 a reserve of land, which created the 17-million-acre Tongass National Forest in 1907, was established and managed by the U. S. Forest Service. Its new rules conflicted with the old, causing confusion, and soon people ignored the laws altogether and cut in trespass.

Alaskan settlers' lumber demands set the territory's timber industry in motion. Federal timber export laws, high freight costs and shipping regulations discouraged exportation, so that the local market grew. Timber was turned into boats, shingles, power poles, pilings, railroad ties, fish trap logs and construction materials. In the 1920s, canneries consumed five million board feet a year just for fish boxes.

Spruce for War Planes

In World Wars I and II, the military selected Alaska's lightweight Sitka spruce for aircraft construction. The Army oversaw its harvest during World War I; during the World War II 1942-1944 Alaska Spruce Log Program, contract loggers cut under the direction of the U. S. Forest Service. Only prime spruce was taken; lower grade woods were left for local mills and non-military projects.

Spruce Log Program jobs, vital to the war effort, saw little turnover,

Courtesy of Tongass Historical Society

Planer, Ketchikan Power Company

and employees needed special permission to leave. Camp life was semi-military. Four floating "A-frame" operations and five shore-based tractor operations towed their logs to the major contractor, Nettleton Logging Company at Edna Bay on Kosciusko Island, where logs were formed into huge rafts of a million or more board feet and towed by tugs to Washington state lumber mills. In comparison, today's average raft holds about a half-million board feet.

By early 1944, metal replaced wood in military aircraft construction and the Alaska Spruce Log Program ended. Within six months, Edna Bay's camp shrank from 250 to 15 people; two months later buildings, equipment and camp were gone.

Hand Logging

There are few stereotypical Paul Bunyan loggers in the woods. The early-day hand logger often was a rugged individualist and outdoorsman with more strength and courage than money, and his was a dangerous job in which the weak, lazy or clumsy seldom survived. Of greenhorn loggers, half might quit, and many others would die in accidents or brawls.

An isolated-hand logger, however, led an agreeable if at times primitive life in the bush. The beginner's investment was small: with axe, saw, sledge hammer, springboards, logging jacks and wedges, he could go to work. If he owned a boat he could live aboard. Or he might camp ashore, perhaps teaming up with an oldtimer to learn the trade in the woods. But long hours together month after month in the woods could be a strain, and disputes carried over to camp could doom a partnership.

Nature provided the logger's table seasonal variety: spring beach greens — raw or wilted with grease, summer berries, and crab apples in the fall. Deer were hunted and venison canned. The ocean provided fresh fish and shellfish. Some gardened to add to staples used for meals of bacon and beans, dried fruit, cornbread, sourdough and regular bread, pancakes and doughnuts. Canned milk was used for many dishes, and "canned cow" was always at hand to add to steaming camp coffee. The strength of camp coffee earned nicknames like "tar," "lye" and "carbide." Bracing as the coffee was, some still longed for stronger stuff. "Alky," "antifreeze" and "tonsil polish" suggest the potency of the brews. During Prohibition, loggers were not above producing a little "snake oil" of their own!

Gyppos, Donkeys and A-Frames

As the number of good hand-logging sites near the shore decreased, mechanical logging increased, allowing logging farther from the beach.

Courtesy of Tongass Historical Society

Head saw, Ketchikan Power Company

Unable to compete against machines, hand loggers laid down their axes, making way for contract "gyppo" loggers who would dominate Southeast logging by 1920.

Animal logging popular elsewhere was little used in Southeast's steep, boggy terrain, although oxen were used near Wrangell around 1906, and horses worked at Union Bay on the Cleveland Peninsula in the late 1920s. The steam engine, or "donkey," with its associated drums and cable was central to early mechanized logging operations and over the years steam, gas and diesel models evolved. "Donkeys" provided the muscle that men lacked to move equipment, rig trees and haul logs out of the woods.

A seafaring man turned logger named Dolbeer built the original "donkey" in the 1880s, and except for substituting wire cable for manila rope, the design was used unchanged through the mid-1930s. At the height of its glory, twenty-six different types of steam donkeys were built in the Pacific Northwest by one firm alone — Willamette Iron Works. Other well known models were produced by other Portland, Seattle and Tacoma companies. The Vulcan, built in Seattle, was said to have "a stronger pull than a New York politician!"

After 1920s surveys showed Alaska timber suitable for pulp and paper production, Deputy Forest Supervisor (later Territorial Governor) B. Frank Heintzleman began a 30-year effort to establish the pulp industry in Southeast Alaska. The first pulp mill built near Juneau in 1920 failed, and the first 50-year Forest Service contracts awarded in 1927 were canceled by the Great Depression. World War II further delayed wood pulp industry development.

The Tongass Timber Act of 1947 allowed timber sales in Alaska to attract foreign investment capital and encourage Territorial growth and employment. In 1951, Ketchikan Pulp Company signed a 50-year contract for 8.25 billion board feet. The mill began operations in April 1954. Pulp mills require great quantities of wood, a demand met more easily by large operations than by the earlier small contract allotments.

Expanded operations of the 1960s added improved roads and heavy equipment. Floating camps grew into communities and family housing was provided in addition to traditional bachelor bunkhouses. Cookhouses, schools, recreational facilities, offices, small stores — perhaps a church — and other services appeared, including radio, telephone and scheduled air taxi flights for rapid transportation and mail service.

Although logging is a large industry, it remains an important small family business for many. While some loggers are schooled for a logging career, many Alaskans have become loggers by living the life, growing up in the camps, and apprenticing with skilled and experienced parents and teachers and models.

Since the turn of the century, technology has advanced the equipment, but harvesting methods remain much the same. The work is as hard as ever in this independent and adventurous lifestyle, and it still takes a special kind of person.

(Courtesy of the Tongass Historical Museum's exhibit and program "Timber-r-r, Logging Life in Southeast Alaska.")

Timber for Pulp: 1954

Ketchikan's settlers depended on the luck of mining and the bounty of Nature's runs of fish for the infant community's economic survival. As the century aged and the town grew to become a city, it became apparent that a broader economic base would be needed. The vast expanses of the Tongass National Forest, created by Congress in 1907, promised to fill the need.

The pioneers, white and Native alike, knew the essential domestic value of their forest products. They used the hemlock, spruce and cedar for construction, for firewood, for fish traps, for ornaments and art. Early records indicate that when they thought of the forest as industry, they thought mainly of paper mills. An early attempt in the 1920s, a U.S. Forest Service timber sale for a paper mill near Juneau, failed. The mill proved too small and lacked ability to compete. Further attempts to utilize forest harvests were aborted by the Depression of the 1930s and then World War II.

The Ketchikan pioneers probably never dreamed that rayon and cellophane would one day be the prime final products of the pulp produced from their vast timberland. The viscose process for making pulp for such products was developed in the 1890s. Norway was the first in production in 1903, followed by a plant in Bangor, Maine. By 1930 the products produced from viscose were being accepted in world markets; by 1950 a viable industry had been established.

Cellophane by mid-century had become a household word. Rayon was a preferred fiber of the textile industry for its resemblance to silk, its ability to take rich, deep dyes, for its draping qualities and its ability — like cotton — to absorb moisture. Rayon's reputation suffered when it was used during World War II as a silk substitute for women's hosiery, which set a new low in high fashion as the stockings sagged to the ankle and bagged elsewhere. It was a misapplication of product to use. Most other industrial uses of rayon are little known — from radiator hoses to fan belts to tires.

After World War II the U.S. Forest Service prepared anew to offer timber in the 17-million-acre Tongass Forest to attract a stable forest products industry to the then-Territory of Alaska. The Tongass Timber bill was passed by Congress and signed by President Harry Truman in 1947. The pen the President used to sign the bill was brought back to Ketchikan by then-Ketchikan Chamber of Commerce manager Bill Boardman.

The Forest Service in 1948 accepted the Ketchikan Pulp and Paper Company (KPC) bid for timber to operate a viscose-process pulp mill at Ward Cove. Ketchikan celebrated!

The 50-year contract for timber cutting rights began in 1954 with the completion of the mill. In the agreement, KPC was granted harvest rights on fewer than a million acres of Tongass Forest lands, mainly on parts of Prince of Wales and Revilla Islands. The acreage amounted to only 4.6 percent of the Tongass National Forest's total acreage.

Today, an untouched 94 percent of the adjusted 16.8-million-acre Tongass Forest still remains closed to logging. Of the open six percent, only a small amount is actually logged in any given year. Second growth in areas logged in the 1950s is already, less than forty years later, being harvested. Alaska's Northern Hemisphere temperate rain forests have proved their hardy regrowth potential and do not suffer the devastation of logged jungle rain forests.

On this six percent of forest land, clearcutting of rotated areas opens the forest floor to sunlight, needed for hemlock and spruce to grow. As many as 15,000 seedlings sprout naturally and quickly on each acre and are then thinned back to about 300, for greater growth potential. Modern forestry techniques include landscape architects who help to lay out timber harvests on these national forest lands to give scenic views due consideration in harvested areas.

Almost 80 percent of Alaska's coastal old growth of ancient trees is totally protected by laws that will allow it to remain that way forever. And there are no endangered species of animals in the Tongass Forest.

Logged by hand logger or by helicopter logger, Alaska's Tongass Forest continues to contribute to the regional and national economy.

Photo by Schallerer/Tongass Historical Society

Limbing, Clarence Purdy's camp, Unuk River

A Manufacturing First: Ketchikan Spruce Mill

The flat 6.5-acre parcel of land that juts out into Tongass Narrows just south of the downtown docks, site of the U. S. Forest Service's new information center, was not always so quietly serene. For more than 80 years a pioneer sawmill groaned and clattered there, soot and ash whirled into the air from its wigwam burner and shrill blasts from its whistle alerted mill workers of starting and quitting time.

Ketchikan Spruce Mill was Alaska's "first manufacturing industry ever established in the north" to utilize a natural resource. (This according to a 1920 issue of the "Pathfinder," a magazine that chronicled the accomplishments of Alaskan pioneers.)

There were three sawmills in the immediate vicinity of Ketchikan as early as 1902. One was at the Indian Village of Saxman three miles south of Ketchikan, but there was no road connection between the two communities until 1925. Another was a Tsimshian Indian enterprise on Gravina Island where Ketchikan's International Airport is now located; it burned in 1904. A third was located at the head of Ward Cove at a small community called Wacker City, where today's Louisiana-Pacific pulp mill and $14 million computerized sawmill now stand.

None of those other early enterprises had a long history. But the downtown spruce mill, which began cutting lumber in 1904, not only survived but became one of the largest plants in Alaska and provided jobs until 1985 when it closed down operations. By 1987 the familiar old mill buildings were torn down and nearby downtowners were able, for the first time, to see the hills of Pennock and Gravina Islands.

The sawmill operation when founded was called Ketchikan Power Company. The mill not only cut wood but supplied power to the city until rivalry with Citizens Power, Light and Water Company prompted the sale of the mill's power division. The company's name was changed in 1923 to Ketchikan Spruce Mills (KSM). The following year a major expansion was under way, which would double the size of the sawmill. When dredging of Thomas Basin began in 1931, KSM was quick to acquire fill material and began to enlarge the size of its tideland property.

The spruce mill was the first completely electrically driven sawmill in Alaska. The power plant consisted of return tubular boilers with dutch oven settings, fired with mill refuse automatically fed from the mill floor. Unacceptable refuse was conveyed to a conical burner, which was a landmark until it was finally taken down in 1969.

In its long years as a major industrial plant, KSM produced lumber for every need, from construction material for a fast-growing community to boards for cannery shooks (fish boxes). Huge "KSM" letters were painted on the major lumber yards in Fairbanks and Anchorage dealing in Ketchikan forest products. In the 1960s huge Japanese lumber ships with rising sun flags called regularly at Ketchikan to load cants of lumber — squared timbers from which dimension lumber would be cut after they reached Japan. In 1967 the mill was sold to Georgia Pacific and in 1985 it closed its doors.

The founder of the mill back in 1903 was H. Z. Burkhart, who built the elegant Queen Anne home at the head of Main Street now owned by the Monrean family. His partner was accountant James J. Daly, who took over management after Burkhart's death in 1909. At Daly's death in 1914, his son Eldon took over. At Eldon's death in the 1940s, his younger brother Milton Daly headed the mill, followed in 1965 by Milton's son John Daly. Mill founder Daly's historic home at 433 Front St. is a landmark atop the tunnel.

It is perhaps appropriate that the pioneer spruce mill site would become the location of the U.S. Forest Service visitor information complex, a showcase for Tongass National Forest resources and products.

Photo by Schallerer/Tongass Historical Society

Ketchikan Spruce Mill, 1940

Ketchikan Pulp Company

Five miles north of Ketchikan, the industrial complex of Ketchikan Pulp Company (KPC) shares the shoreline arc of Ward Cove with a picturesque cannery-on-stilts, Ward Cove Packing. The serene waters of the cove float Ketchikan Pulp's log rafts and the occasional huge, salt-battered freighter moored to load bales of pulp; in season the waters also ripple with the brisk traffic of the cannery's colorful fleet of small fishing boats. Flocks of gulls perch on KPC logs and bald eagles on nearby trees, their sharp eyes watching for the flicker of resident fish or offal from the cannery.

The historic cannery and the modern pulp mill represent the two prime pillars of Ketchikan's economic base: Fisheries created the frontier city; utilization of the region's timber products supported the expansion and survival of the present community.

Ketchikan Pulp Company's plant is not the stereotypical "paper mill" with acrid, sulfurous effluvium. Some $45 million has been spent since the mill's construction in 1954 on both air and water quality controls to render the industry compatible with today's strict environmental standards.

KPC produces high grade dissolving pulp which is used not only in the manufacture of rayon, today's high fashion cousin of silk, but for rayon cord tires, carpets, drapes and cellophane food packaging. Its specialty products are pharmaceutical goods, dietary food additives, sponges, furniture lacquers and dice.

The filters in cigarettes are made of a pulp product called "tow," pronounced "toe" — and it's biodegradable. The pure, natural pulp made primarily of Alaska's rain forest hemlock is used as "fiber" in over-the-counter laxatives. It is the smoothing ingredient in ice cream that prevents this popular dessert from becoming icy. It is the stuff of sterile absorbent materials used by surgeons in operating rooms.

And it was pulp — the jobs it created, and the mill's substantial year-round contribution to Ketchikan's economy — that changed Ketchikan from a town to a city. It changed forested Prince of Wales Island to the west of Ketchikan from an outpost of subsidized, isolated villages to a prosperous logging region of Southern Southeast Alaska.

From the earliest days of its history, Alaska looked to settlement to ensure its future. Ketchikan Pulp Company, beginning in 1952, brought in tax-paying workers and their families, first for construction of the $54 million facility and then in 1954 for residence. Approximately a thousand year-round jobs resulted, including positions at the mill and at the KPC sawmills and logging camps, amounting today to a $5 million monthly payroll.

That is the economic picture. The civic and social picture was just as important. Congressional passage of the Tongass Timber Bill in 1947 to allow the U. S. Forest Service authority to negotiate a 50-year timber cutting contract with Ketchikan Pulp Company was the first step in the

Photo by Paul Saari/Tongass Historical Society

(Clockwise from Left): Ketchikan Pulp Co., Salmon Byproducts Corporation, Ward Cove Packing Company, 1954

transformation of Ketchikan. Anticipating the influx of workers and their families and their need for homesites, the Forest Service cut new roads into forest-bound land north of the city and expanded those, and existing roads, with spurs. Scenic beach lots and upland view lots were created. Sites were reserved for schools, churches and public use.

Residential homesites were cleared farther up hillsides above the city. Highrise apartment complexes were built on the West End of town. Other apartment buildings were built near the city center. Single-family home construction was a busy trade in every section of the community. A new high school was built in 1954 and within a decade a new elementary and a junior high school joined the school district's facilities.

Logging activity began at sites on Prince of Wales Island, creating "instant communities." At one time KPC's Thorne Bay camp and community was documented as the "10th largest city in Alaska."

As the town, and its tax base, grew, recreation improvements were made at Rotary Beach south of the city and at the popular picnic grounds at Ward Lake north of town. Roads and trails were improved at Totem Bight park and at Saxman Indian village's totem park. Parking areas were expanded at popular marina and boat launching sites.

Since the mill began operations in 1954, much of the early excitement and impact of the industry has been forgotten. "Mill workers" have blended into the community and become just "Ketchikan people." For many years the town's posters, announcements and sometimes school projects have been lettered or drawn on sheets of pulp. Today's exciting Fourth of July Logging Show, a festival of bucking, sawing, axe-throwing and other logging skills, attracts KPC loggers.

Ketchikan Pulp Company is part of the community in other important ways — willing to sponsor a sports team, to sponsor the church directory in the daily newspaper, the first to donate and contribute to the city's many activities. KPC is an integral part of Ketchikan.

KPC: A View from the Bleachers

By Roland Stanton

I was an aspiring chemical engineering student in 1948 when a contract for a timber sale between Ketchikan Pulp Company (KPC) and the U.S. Forest Service was signed. I didn't know at the time that I would one day move to Ketchikan to work at the Ward Cove KPC pulp mill or that over the years of residency I would become a member of the Gateway Borough Assembly. I especially didn't anticipate at the time that my wife, Alaire, would become not only president of the Ketchikan School Board, but, in time, mayor of Ketchikan.

In 1948, Ketchikan Pulp Company was a jointly owned venture held by American Viscose and Puget Sound Pulp and Timber. American Viscose had been put together by Philadelphia financial interests when they bought out several British-owned rayon makers in 1940. At that time, of course, the Battle of Britain was under way, the Nazis were expected to invade England, the United States was not yet in the war, and the British were hard-pressed for money. So $7 billion dollars' worth of British stock was sold in New York in order to buy munitions for their war effort.

Puget Sound Pulp and Timber under President Lawson P. Turcotte was the most innovative producer of pulp in the world. The company not only produced the industry's cleanest pulp, it was a pioneer in developing new pulp products.

When other pulp companies were pouring waste "process liquor" down the drain into the sewers, Turcotte's company was making money selling liquor-based products it developed. One of those products was an additive for drilling mud used in oil exploration and recovery. Another was synthetic, or imitation, vanilla used for flavoring. Because other pulp mills routinely dumped what they unknowingly considered "waste" liquor, and in huge quantities, Puget Sound Pulp kept its innovative liquor products secret. Some of them made in the Bellingham plant were shipped to Calgary, Canada, and sold from there to protect their source.

Turcotte and others in the industry were well aware of the Alaska timber resource and the potential of harvesting and utilizing the vast amounts of over-ripe timber rotting in Southeast's Tongass Forest. They knew the Forest Service had been working for years to bring the pulp industry to Alaska; the plan almost came to fruition in the late 1920s but the Great Depression blocked its completion.

So in 1947, anticipating approval of the 1948 timber sale, Puget Sound Pulp and Timber recruited American Viscose to join them in the Tongass venture — one, because Puget Sound needed capital and two, because American Viscose needed a supplier.

About this time, Weyerhaeuser Timber Company was developing a method of making pulp in a process based on magnesia instead of lime rock. This would make it possible to burn the liquor produced in pulp cooking and get heat and chemicals from it. When de-barked wood chips are cooked, the "brown stuff" — the binding which holds the wood fibers together in a tree — is dissolved. This problem waste, or liquor, is thickened in the magnesia-based sulfite process so that it evaporates and burns. The heat from the burning could supply 60 percent of the total energy needed to run the mill. Another 20 percent of energy could come from burning the waste bark and sawdust, leaving only 20 percent to be fired by oil.

Ketchikan Pulp mill became the first built to use this new process.

Pulp mills also require a lot of water, so for the new Ketchikan mill an 85-foot-high concrete dam was built in the Ward Creek valley, utilizing and expanding Lake Connell. The lake holds about 60 days of water and Ketchikan's usually dependably heavy rains plus the snow on the mountains allow the lake to maintain a 90- to 100-day supply.

Twenty million gallons a day are treated to high grade drinking water standards and another 17 million gallons are filtered for less demanding uses. At the time Ketchikan's pulp mill was built, that would have supplied the city of Tacoma, Washington, with a population of more than 100,000 — and its leading industry, a pulp mill.

It was at the parent plant in Bellingham in 1953 that I came into the picture. I was among several chemical engineers hired to operate a miniature pulp mill to determine the best way to build it, using a new process and a wood from a new area — Alaska. I spent my time bleaching with machinery about the size of a clothes washer. It stirred and it spun, and we went through five separate bleaches with different conditions each day. On one side of us were chemical engineers cooking the wood, and on the opposite side others were making rayon. We spent nine months at the discovery process before we headed north for Ketchikan to start up the mill.

The start-up was bedlam. As soon as we cooked the first pulp and the stuff hit the wash plant, it started to foam. There was foam everywhere. For weeks I spent my time with little pumps, pumping foam from serious to less serious places, wearing rubber boots and rain gear. When we beat the foam problem, the wash plant began to deteriorate, plus a lot of pipes. After much study and work we determined that the salt from the sea water in which the logs were towed to us was causing the attack on all our stainless steel. The solution was major replacement with stainless steel with a higher molybdenum content.

We were a new industry in a new place, trying new woods, water and techniques. In time the bugs were worked out and the mill settled into doing what it is supposed to, the way it is supposed to do it. From then on, our job was to make refinements and modifications to make the mill what it is today — modern, environmentally safe and productive.

(*Roland Stanton spent 22 years with KPC, leaving the company in 1975. He is now the sexton of the City of Ketchikan's Bayview Cemetery.*)

Tourists Are Delightful People

By June Allen

Tourists and travel writers have been visiting Ketchikan almost from the day of the city's incorporation back in 1900. In those days they arrived on steamships, stepped daintily across the plank dock and strolled the wooden streets in high button shoes to gaze at totem poles, glance askance at the notorious red-light district of Creek Street, observe the salmon canneries, crane their necks to watch the soaring flight of eagles, and leave with a trinket or two in their luggage.

Secretary of State William Henry Seward, who negotiated the Purchase of Alaska from Russia in 1867, was a tourist. One of his stops was with the Tlingit Indians at Tongass Island in 1868, before there was a Ketchikan. Presbyterian missionary Sheldon Jackson came first to Alaska as a tourist, in a series of voyages that prompted him to devote his life to Alaska's Native people. President Warren G. Harding visited Ketchikan in 1923, dedicated the Masonic Temple that was located where today's State Building now stands, and had the honor of having three Ketchikan streets named after him — Warren Street, G Street, and Harding Street. President Franklin Delano Roosevelt made a secret wartime tour in 1944, although he probably bypassed Ketchikan.President Jerry Ford went fishing here in 1990 while Betty had a Monte Cristo sandwich at the Ketchikan Cafe.

John Wayne was a regular visitor to Ketchikan in the 1960s, arriving in his yacht, the *Wild Goose*. Also to have strolled Ketchikan streets shortly after were bandleader Harry James, ventriloquist Edgar Bergen (Candace Bergen/Murphy Brown's famous father), an aloof Cary Grant, movie star Alice Faye and her bandleader husband, the feisty Phil Harris, who got in a shouting match on Creek Street over the Canadian money exchange at a tourist shop.

More recently there have been visits from Roy Rogers and Dale Evans and their extensive family, and Greer Garson. Jonathan Winters fished at Waterfall Resort on Prince of Wales Island and Patrick Swayze caused some heart flutters when he appeared unexpectedly at Ketchikan's Plaza Port West mall some seasons ago.

Tourists today arrive on airplanes, on the Alaska State ferries and via the cruise ships that call two, three and four at a time at Ketchikan's downtown docks and harbor from May through September — a quarter of a million cruise ship visitors each year. They are vacationing, having a wonderful time and enjoying every minute of sharing Ketchikan's unique lifestyle — even the rain.

What is it that tourists find so unique, that often prompts them to say that Ketchikan is their favorite port of call?

First, it is the fact that Ketchikan is not a theme-park tourist destination. It is a prosperous, busy, year-round city whose residents welcome visitors to share their town with them. Second, it is the friendliness and helpfulness of the residents. Third, it is the uniqueness of Ketchikan's rain-forest location, abundance of fish and tides.

Ketchikan's 20-foot tides startle visitors the most, whether they come from inland hometowns or communities familiar with the ocean. This awe is summarized in a question by one serious gentleman, who examined the barnacles and other marine life attached to dockside piling as he climbed the steep ramp — it was low tide at the time — to the dock. "I noticed the...ocean life on those poles, and it appears the water level was higher at some time in the past," he said. "Was it?" [Well, yes it was — about six hours before! And would be again in another six hours.]

Courtesy of Tongass Historical Society

S.S. *Princess Royal*

Another gentleman, arriving on one of the smaller cruise ships tied up at low tide, was annoyed as he clambered onto the dock. "Why do you people build your docks so high!" he said. "Our cabin window overlooks the piling!" He didn't listen to an explanation of tides but he was gracious enough to come back later, when the tide had floated his cabin well above the dock, to say he saw why.

Two women made interesting remarks as they returned to their ship at high tide after hours of shopping in town. One stopped in surprise as she recognized her own cruise line and said, "Well, will you look at that! When we got off, it was on our floor. Now we have to go back on in the basement." Said the other, "How do you suppose they do that?"

Possibly the best story was about an independent tourist who arrived by plane, and was so eager to begin his adventure that the first thing he did was to rent a skiff to do a little fishing. Not wanting to miss a thing, he later tied the skiff to a piling and climbed a ladder to the dock to do a little sightseeing. When he returned some hours later — and there was a group of locals waiting to see the fun — the skiff was hanging by its painter, dangling above the water. The man was shocked. "Didn't you know the tide goes out around here?" asked one local. "Well, yes," the visitor said indignantly. "But I didn't know it went down!"

A British visitor familiar with literature but not with Alaska's flora asked seriously if the Tongass Forest hemlock was what Socrates used to commit suicide. Another asked, "Which way to the Tongass Forest?" even though he had been sailing through part of the 17-million-acre forest for hours. An obvious city dweller from New Jersey was stunned to see children eating salmonberries along Ketchikan Creek's bank. "Do you eat them," he asked timidly, "right off...the bush?"

Visitors know fish are part and parcel of Ketchikan. One woman, gazing out over Tongass Narrows one windy morning, asked what the white things on the water were. Whitecaps, she was told. "Oh, are they good to eat?" she asked.

Visitors leaning over the railings of Ketchikan Creek, watching the migration of salmon upstream, are sometimes baffled by the habits and nature of fish. One man, observing the "burp bubbles" of milling fish, exclaimed, "Good heavens, they're burping little oil slicks!"

And finally, a couple was approaching the Tongass Historical Museum and saw the big banner "Museum." The man said, cynically, "Oh. They have a museum here. From the looks of the place, I thought they still used everything."

Maybe that's the charm of Ketchikan. Except for widened and paved streets, it looks pretty much like it did 50 years ago. And will 50 years from now.

CONCERNING BOOTLEGGING.

(Stroller's Weekly.)

Any official, Federal or Territorial, who puts forth honest effort to stamp out the bootlegging evil that now flourishes rampant in this and other parts of the country is entitled to the aid, support and backing of all good people we care not what his politics may be.

Locally it is an off week when illicit whiskey does not claim a victim and this condition of affairs is common knowledge and has been common knowledge for a long time. And conditions are growing worse instead of better. Lack of prosecution has emboldened those engaged in the illicit traffic until it is carried on almost as openly as when there were licensed bars. It is claimed that much of the stuff that is being sold and guzzled around in this portion of the Territory bears little, if any, semblance to real whisky but are poisonous decoctions that mean certain death to those who persistently indulge in them—rank poison that pegs the victim who stays with it as surely as does the bite of a rattlesnake.

The mania for making and drinking home brew is another evil which, if persisted in, will do as much toward weakening and destroying those who persist in it as will the indiscriminate drinking of moonshine of which it is a near relative. More than that. Any community that contracts the home-brew habit is bound to deteriorate into semi-idiocy and imbecility, the marks of which will be more apparent in the future generations than in the present, for the sins of home brew addicts are bound to be apparent in their offspring. It is a law of nature and there is no side-stepping it.

In view of existing conditions, therefore, we say all honor and all hail to any one or set of officials who will abolish the flagrant violations of the laws of the land and remove the death-dealing menace that is hovering like an unclean thing over the country—making a joke of law, filling our cemeteries with its victims and stamping the brand of imbecility on children yet unborn.

If the laws as they now stand on our statute books can not be enforced, let us advocate the return of the open saloon with all their degeneracy, their vice and their damning influence. They were palaces of goodness compared with their successors.

Courtesy of Tongass Historical Society

Ketchikan Alaska Chronicle, September 16, 1921

THE ROARING TWENTIES

Rumrunners and Prohibition

Laws forbidding intoxicants were part of Alaska's history from the beginning. The Russian-America Company managers prohibited alcohol in The Company's American holdings and frowned on the Yankee traders who used the demon rum as a trade item with Alaska's Natives. After the U. S. Purchase of Alaska in 1867, military administration of the vast northern territory continued the legal ban on alcoholic beverages.

Farther north, hidden stills and crocks of home brew supplied any needs of the sparse population during those early years. Ketchikan, however, is only 90 miles north of the British Columbia port of Prince Rupert, which made the smuggling of good Canadian booze easy work. Enforcement of the dry law was difficult, because Ketchikan's small-boat rumrunners were familiar with every cove and inlet on the run from Prince Rupert to Ketchikan and easily evaded detection.

Ketchikan's turn-of-the-century commercial businesses were built with contraband liquor storage in mind. Many had trap doors in their floors, allowing skiffs to maneuver through the under-city piling on proper tides to deliver shipments. Others had dumb-waiters to lift the bottles to upper stories for storage. Some early homes, too, had "dry bars" behind hidden panels.

After Alaska was granted Territorial status and laws in 1912, the ban on liquor was lifted. Private stocks in card rooms, drug stores and tobacco shops were no longer necessary, and saloons opened their doors along Ketchikan's busy Front Street.

Sentiments against alcoholic beverages were spreading across the nation, however, during those first two decades of the new century. Groups such as the Women's Christian Temperance Union were lobbying for prohibition of liquor, and newspapers made a celebrity of axe-swinging, saloon-hacking Carry Nation. There was a fear that World War I doughboys would come home from Europe with a taste for French wines.

The U. S. Congress bowed to lobby pressure and passed the 18th Amendment to the Constitution, the Volstead Act that prohibited the manufacture, sale or transportation of liquor. It was submitted to the States for ratification in December 1917. Congress then passed the Bone Dry law for the Territories, including Alaska, even before the 18th Amendment was finally ratified by the States in January 1919.

Photo by Winter & Pond/Alaska Historical Library

Camp Moonshine

The Bone Dry law presented only minor problems in Ketchikan, already equipped and experienced in rumrunning. Ketchikan's proximity to Prince Rupert and Canadian liquors made it a center for a lucrative bootlegging industry. Prohibition also boosted business at the brothels on Creek Street where liquor had always been available in spite of any restrictive laws.

Rumrunners would slip into coves on Pennock Island and wait for tides to allow deliveries to waiting trap doors in the city. Gunny sacks full of bottles would be stashed in the water near Mountain Point at high tide, to await pickup at low tide.

Oldtimers remember spying on loads of bottles being unloaded and stored under cover of darkness in shacks and sheds at the edge of town, only to be lifted later the same night by rival operators. Children would collect empty bottles floating on morning tides and sell them back to bootleggers.

The "Dry Squad," the nicknamed enforcement arm of the new law, was obviously aware of the extent of illegal traffic in liquor to Ketchikan, which was Alaska's largest city at the time and gateway to the rest of the Territory.

The Coast Guard Cutter *Bothwell* was sent to Ketchikan early in 1921, perhaps as a warning of what was to come, but continued on to other duty. The Cutter *Smith* was assigned to Ketchikan January 1, 1923, followed later in the year by the Cutter *Cygan,* one of only two armed vessels assigned to Alaska's waters.

One of President Franklin Delano Roosevelt's campaign promises was an end to Prohibition. That became reality in December 1933. First beer became legal in Alaska, and later, liquor sales were allowed. Creek Street's illegal and unlicensed sales of booze continued without interruption. And Coast Guard cutters continued to be stationed in Ketchikan — although duties changed once Prohibition was a thing of the past.

The Cow's Tale

During the Roaring Twenties, while rumrunners were slipping easily along the Alaska shorelines with their cargos of illegal liquor, one Ketchikan family was troubled by the logistics of a different type of voyage they were facing: taking their cow to be bred.

There was (and is) no agriculture in Ketchikan, but there were dairies in various locations in the first fifty years or so of the town's history, one on Pennock Island, directly across Tongass Narrows from downtown Ketchikan.

Pharmacist Bob Race, son of pioneer Ketchikan pharmacist Harry Race, tells of a period in his 1920's boyhood when the family moved to remote Square Island north of Ketchikan to a fox farm. It was an idyllic location to rear children, but the grandparents down south worried about the family's having no milk.

So they shipped up a cow.

In time the cow went dry and then the logistic planning began to find a way to haul her from Square Island to Ketchikan to be bred. They loaded her on a scow and as they neared the dairy on Pennock Island, they wondered how they were going to get that seasick cow off the scow and onto dry land. But the cow heard the voice of the bull in the distance, jumped off the scow and swam to the island.

There is the romance of the sea and of early dairy farming in the heart of this tale.

Courtesy of Tongass Historical Society

New United States Lighthouse Service Depot — now U.S. Coast Guard Base, Ketchikan

Courtesy of Tongass Historical Society

L.H.S. Tender *Fern* at old U.S.L.H.S. Depot, Ketchikan

Bill Lattin/Courtesy of Don "Bucky" Dawson

L.H.S. Tender, *Cedar*

Lighthouse Service to Coast Guard

The Klondike Gold Rush of 1898 was responsible for a number of events in Alaska, most notably the focusing of world attention on the remote territory on the northwest shoulder of the North American continent. There was no one, either those with feet itching to travel or those content to abide at home, who hadn't noticed at least slight symptoms of gold fever. This applied to the U. S. Congress as well.

Whalers, steamship companies and fish cannery interests had previously lobbied unsuccessfully for lighthouses along Alaska's treacherous shorelines. But when newspaper editors took up the standard, along with stories about the fabulous gold rush, Congress was willing to listen, and act.

Funding was approved in 1900 for the first two of Alaska's lighthouses completed in 1902, one north and one south of Juneau. The third was Mary Island Light Station, requested as early as 1890, and finally completed in 1903. Mary Island is located in Revillagigedo Channel just south of Ketchikan, the gateway to Alaska. To the north of Ketchikan is the landmark Guard Island light station built in 1904, which marks the Clarence Strait entrance into Tongass Narrows. Guard Island's old light is displayed at the Ketchikan Historical Museum.

Other light station construction followed. In 1910 Congress created the 16th Lighthouse District in Alaska, which would receive funds to pay lightkeepers and provide a tender for navigational aids. Ketchikan became the district's depot in 1918, with its first quarters where today's Talbot's Building Supplies is located, and was assigned the tenders *Rose* and *Cedar*.

In 1912 land was obtained for the Lighthouse Depot south of town where the Coast Guard base is now located and in 1919 buildings were constructed there. When the first Coast Guard cutters were assigned to Ketchikan in 1923, they moored near City Float. In 1939 the Lighthouse Service and U. S. Coast Guard merged. Coast Guard operations began at the new base in 1940.

During World War II Base Ketchikan served as a transit and staging area for the rest of Alaska's theater of war. Wartime mobilization brought Ketchikan's military complement to 750 people. After the war, by the late 1960s all Alaska's light stations were automated.

Today the base is Southeast Alaska's largest military installation with more than 200 personnel. It is the primary source of industrial services for all Alaska Coast Guard units, responsible for construction and repair of navigational aids, shipyard maintenance for 110-foot cutters and smaller vessels, installation and repair of electronics equipment, and servicing automated lighthouses. In addition, it is responsible for search and rescue and law enforcement operations in Southeastern.

The Guard Island Tale

Before automation, lighhouses in Alaska were manned by conscientious keepers who kept an eye on whatever happened in their range of sight. In the late 1920s a man named George West was keeper of the light on Guard Island, just north of Ketchikan. During his absences, Mrs. West filled in for him.

Once she was witness to a robbery and murder which she observed through binoculars as she watched the maneuvering fishing fleet off the mainland of Cleveland Peninsula. While watching a fish buyer's boat, she saw a man murder the buyer, then try to rob the safe on the boat where the money to buy fish was kept. The culprit was apprehended. They say strands of the murdered man's hair were found under the accused man's fingernails.

The Lincoln Rock Tale

The original Lincoln Rock lighthouse station was destroyed by a storm in 1912. The lonely keeper was rescued from the upper story of the light after the storm, but he was found to be insane and died shortly thereafter. Which perhaps proves that the weather here can drive a person over the edge.

GETTING AROUND

On Land, on Sea and in the Air
By Ralph A. Bartholomew

(The late Ralph A. Bartholomew, pioneer and owner of Ireland Transfer & Storage Company, wrote this article for the magazine that accompanied the dedication of Ketchikan International Airport in 1973. It is reprinted with permission of his son Ralph M. Bartholomew.)

I came to Alaska in 1915 on the tender *Chacon* for Fidalgo Island Packing. In fact, my brother Sam was captain of the boat. And I've been around the waterfront ever since and watched Ketchikan grow.

All other transportation in the early days was on the water. Every freighter was a passenger ship, too, and there were a lot of good ones and some bad ones. One nice thing about them was that they had to unload their cargo at every port so the passengers had plenty of time to stroll around and see the town.

The average ships that serviced Alaska were cast-offs from the Pacific Coast runs. There were lots of ships but most of them were small and they went long distances farther north, clear to the Westward, so a round trip took two weeks or more. And most of them ended up on a rock somewhere or ended up as scrap.

In fact, a great many rocks were named after ships that went down after hitting them. Idaho Rock off Saxman was named after the ship that went down there. We had some close calls near to home, too. *The City of Seattle* went aground at Sunny Point right in town (near today's ferry terminal), but didn't tip over — floated her off at high tide. And the *Northwest* of Alaska Steam went aground on Pennock Island once.

There were a lot of ships. Independent Steamship Company had the *Humboldt* with Captain Baughman. Pacific Coast Steamship had *The City of Seattle* and *The City of Spokane*. That outfit was taken over by Pacific Steamship and we had the *Dorothy Alexander* up here. There was a fleet of the Admiral Line, too, the "Admiral This" and the "Admiral That". And Canadian steamships, too.

Then there was the Alaska Transportation Company with the *Zapora*. My brother was captain of that when he died. She was an old halibut boat, a big one. She was converted into a passenger ship and freighter. They also had the old *Washington*.

There were some ships that weren't so good, too, like the *Alki* and the *Dispatch*. You could come up from Seattle for $12 to $15 but it took four days. The fare on a good boat was from $25 to $35.

Transportation here in town during the first years I was here was on foot over two plank walks — one along the water and one up on the hill, about where Second Avenue is now. There were maybe half a dozen cars. And one motorcycle, owned by Lawrence Erickson who worked at Ketchikan Meat Company with me in 1915. My biggest thrill was to get to deliver meat to the canneries on that motorcycle.

Gene Wacker built himself a bus and ran a stage line to Wacker City which was at Ward Cove about where the pulp mill is now.

In 1916 they put a plank road into Newtown (around the outside of what today is the tunnel) just wide enough for two small cars to pass. The mayor, Mike Heneghan, led the parade to celebrate the street opening in one of the few cars in town. Then when Standard Oil came in, the road to the south was built out to their plant and later when the Coast Guard base moved south (1919) the road was extended out there. It was just wide enough for McBane's delivery wagon.

The first plane that came to Ketchikan was in 1922 and people have been crazy about flying ever since. In fact, I was one of the first airline agents that took my pay in free rides in the airplane! Most of the flying in those early days was for joy rides or cannery people getting to their canneries or checking salmon runs or traps or things of that nature.

When Pan Am came in (1936-38) the planes used to knock out the floats at City Float so they moved out to Ward Cove. Had to take a skiff out to the float to board there. About that time I was on a committee to find a place for a Ketchikan airfield. Most of the places we studied back then were the same places studied in the late '60s when plans were made for the present Ketchikan International Airport. Larry Hagen, George Beck and I took Army Major Nold around and showed him all the places.

When we took him over to Metlakatla, he saw all that flat country with those "beaver ponds" and he decided that was the right spot. "All we have to do is fill it in," he said. Well, he never worked in muskeg before. Some of it was 25 to 30 feet deep and he found he had to scrape it all out and fill in. Finally they knocked a mountain down to fill the field in. The CCC boys and Army engineers and others built it.

Now we've got our own airport (on Gravina Island). Guess we'll always be crazy about flying here.

Photo by Sixten Johanson/Tongass Historical Society

Star of Greenland **at Cape Chacon, 1923**

Steering for Alaska

The first ships to ply Alaska's waters, from the multi-national explorers in the 1700s through the whaling and other commercial ventures of the 1800s, were sailing ships. Russian supply ships hoisted sail from Siberian ports to the Russian-American settlements in Alaska and returned with cargos of fur pelts from the late 1700s until the 1867 U. S. Purchase of Alaska.

Wind power was the first motive power of the cannery interests that steered for Alaska after the Purchase, and for the mail and supply vessels accommodating as well the occasional prospector or scientific party. Even into the 1920s the energy-efficient windjammers boasting huge hold capacity were still carrying freight and labor north and lucrative cannery packs south.

But by the 1870s more weather-reliable coastal steamers had replaced the windjammers for general travel to Alaska. In those years, weekly freight and mail runs from Portland, Oregon, with passenger service included, were being made to Sitka, Alaska's first capital. (The capital move to Juneau was begun in 1900.)

North Sea Photo by Schallerer/Tongass Historical Society

Courtesy of Tongass Historical Society

S.S. *Alaska* in Tongass Narrows

It was the Klondike Gold Rush of 1898 that made Alaska's waterways world-famous. Alaska Steamship Company had begun regular freight and passenger service to Alaska as early as 1895, and was joined in the prosperous gold-fever years that followed by others, most notably the Admiral Line and later the Northern Steamship Line plus other smaller enterprises of shorter service duration.

Without agriculture and manufacturing, almost everything Alaska's few residents needed had to be freighted in. And there were the gold cleanups and the salmon packs for return trips.

By mid-century, the profit margin of Alaska Steam, the enduring and only remaining steamship line to Alaska, was being nibbled away by growing post-war airline competition and the opening to public use of the wartime Alaska (Alcan) Highway. Alaska Steam's passenger service was discontinued at the end of the tourist season in 1954 with the final sailing of the *Denali* and freight service ended in 1968 with the final run of the *Fortuna*.

Wings Replace Sails and Steam

The airplane came into its own in Alaska shortly after the end of World War I. It was in 1922 that Ketchikan's Roy Jones landed on Tongass Narrows with his flying boat the Northbird. And it was just that, a flying boat — no wheels, no floats, simply a double wing with a push-prop engine mounted on the hull of a boat.

With this machine, and the enthusiastic support of the entire community, Jones began the first commercial air service in all of Alaska. In addition to joy rides, the Northbird carried businessmen to their canneries and to check salmon runs, prospectors over likely terrain, sportsmen to remote lakes, and freight to isolated camps and communities.

But while the prospects were good, the weather was bad, the technology new and the financing shaky. The sporadic service came to an end in less than two years.

In 1936 Ketchikan aviation came into its own when pioneer Alaskan aviator Bob Ellis established enduring bush pilot service in Ketchikan, Ellis Air Transport, serving the city and outlying communities — and making occasional runs to Seattle. Ellis' operation eventually merged with Alaska Airlines in 1968. The Ellis twin goose emblem still is affixed to the Tongass Avenue building that was the air taxi terminal, even though it now houses a restaurant.

In 1938 Pan American World Airways began Clipper flights from Seattle to Southeastern Alaska, including Ketchikan, after two years of trial runs. It had a short lifespan, the service interrupted by logistic and weather problems, plus gathering war clouds. World War II prompted the building of a military airfield on Annette Island, 17 miles south of Ketchikan.

Photo by Schallerer/Courtesy of Don "Bucky" Dawson

First Seattle to Ketchikan route survey flight of Pan Am's Sikorsky S-42B flying boat Clipper, City Float, 1938

Photo by Schallerer/Courtesy of Don "Bucky" Dawson

Receiving express mail from Pan Am clipper flight are (from left to right): Emmett Ryus, J. Johnson, George Beck, Captain John Mattis, Ralph Bartholomew, and Larry Hagen.

From war's end until 1973 when Ketchikan's own airport was built on adjacent Gravina Island, Annette served Ketchikan's air traffic needs. In those years, Ketchikan passengers flew by Grumman Goose or PBYs to Annette, where they boarded prop planes, and later jets, south or northbound.

Pan Am made scheduled stops at Annette at the end of World War II. In 1955 Pacific Northern began regular service, merging with Western in 1967. Western service was suspended by the CAB in 1972 and Alaska Airlines became Ketchikan's carrier.

Photo by Schallerer/Courtesy of Don "Bucky" Dawson

Ellis started in 1936 with the biplane at right, Ellis Air Transport, 1940

The State Ferries

Island-bound Ketchikan had long hoped either for a road connection to the mainland or car-ferry service to Washington state. During the 1930s there was talk of a leg of an "international highway" that would follow British Columbia's coastline — allowing the possibility of bridge connection from the other side of Revilla Island to the mainland. Those hopes were dashed in 1942 when that suggested route was moved far inland and became the rapidly built, war-emergency military Alcan, or Alaska Highway.

But the wish for car ferries, expressed as soon as Henry Ford's first vehicles made their initial appearances on early Ketchikan plank streets, was pressed forward. The first Legislature of the new State of Alaska acted promptly in 1959 to find a way to fill Southeastern Alaska's transportation vacuum. In 1963 the first three of the eight Alaska state ferries were on line, carrying people, cars and freight between Southeastern ports and to Washington state.

There are at least two routes now for Ketchikan travel — by air or by water, with the family vehicle — or a shipping van — on a state ferry's car deck.

Courtesy of Ketchikan Daily News

Alaska Marine Highway ferry, M/V *Columbia*

WORLD WAR II

Blackouts and Enemy Spies

Ketchikan was as outraged as every other American city when the Japanese bombed Pearl Harbor December 7, 1941. A Ketchikan boy, Navy Ensign Irvin Thompson, 24, was among the 2,300 dead in that attack, lost in the sinking of the battleship *Oklahoma*. Men lined up at Main and Dock Streets that very day to join the military.

Within hours the United States declared war on the Axis powers: Germany, Italy, and Japan — the enemy already suspected of spying in Alaska waters. A Japanese radio operator at the Craig cannery was said to have disappeared after hearing news of Pearl Harbor. A spy at Waterfall cannery was rumored to have been evacuated by Japanese submarine under cover of night. There were reported sub sightings all along the west coast of Prince of Wales Island.

In a matter of weeks it became clear that World War II might come perilously close to Ketchikan. The Annette military airfield had been under construction during the year. Coast Guard Base Ketchikan was a logical target for the enemy. A few families sent wives and children south along with the families being evacuated from the north in blacked out ships.

Civil defense teams were organized and air raid practices held in Ketchikan. Radio silence was a signal for total blackout. Sand and water barrels were placed on rooftops in case of incendiary attack. Windows were covered at night and businesses built plywood blackout double-door entrances to their shops. Watchmen patrolled the streets to make sure no light was showing.

Ketchikan was a city of 5,000 when war broke out. The supply of housing, then as now, never met the demand. The ranks at Annette and Base Ketchikan swelled. Army Engineers from Annette slept on the docks. A USO center next to City Float on Water Street was equipped. Local businesses donated records for dancing, stationery for letters home and other furnishings. Young women attended USO dances and served as hostesses. High school students took classes in Morse code and semaphore signals.

Men too young and too old for military service practiced with armory firearms at the rifle range north of town. They also manned the fishing fleet, some boys hardly old enough to shave serving as skippers of fishing boats.

Ketchikan's young men were gone to war. At the time of the Pearl Harbor attack, the Ketchikan unit of the Alaska National Guard's 297th Infantry had already joined other Alaska units in training at Chilkoot Barracks at Haines, north of Juneau at the head of Lynn Canal. Many of those men were sent to duty posts at other locations in Alaska.

When the Japanese bombed Alaska's Dutch Harbor and invaded and occupied two of the Aleutian Islands, beginning in June of 1942, war emergency preparedness in Alaska reached a fever pitch. The Aleutians were the doorway to invasion of the mainland and enemy control of Alaska waters.

For some reason, any news of the war in Alaska — after that first public announcement of the Japanese bombing of Dutch Harbor — was under a news blackout by the military. The rest of the nation was unaware that all of the then-Territory of Alaska was a theater of war and its troop movements top secret. While newspaper headlines screamed advances and retreats in the South Pacific, there was no coverage of the battles raging in Alaska.

Perhaps it was because the Alaska theater engagements were the only World War II battles ever fought on the North American continent, on American soil. That knowledge could have caused unparalleled panic in the United States.

Because of that news blackout, most Americans are unaware of what is sometimes called "The Forgotten War" in Alaska. And yet it was pivotal in America's victory in the Pacific in World War II. The Japanese themselves debated over whether or not to divide their forces between Alaska and the South Pacific. They decided on the two-pronged attack. A year after the first attack, the enemy was driven out of Alaska. Had the enemy aborted the Alaska campaign, the results of the war might have been different.

Ketchikan was 1,000 miles away from those battles that raged over a 1,000-mile stretch of the Aleutian Islands. But its men served there. Its forests provided the lumber for military construction, its gray-painted boats provided a mosquito fleet in support of military.

The war is not forgotten in Ketchikan.

Relocation and Internment

From 1941 to 1945, during the United States' involvement in World War II, American casualties would be listed at 292,131 dead and 115,185 wounded.

Those numbers of "dead" probably do not include the several dozen Aleuts, resident victims of the Japanese invasion and occupation of two of Alaska's Aleutian Islands. A few were butchered on the spot, others died slow deaths in Japanese prison camps. The figures of the "dead" and "wounded" do not include the hundreds, perhaps more, Aleut citizens of the United States who were removed from their Aleutian homes and relocated to internment camps in other parts of Alaska.

The "wounded" statistics also do not include the thousands of Japanese-American citizens from California to Alaska who suffered similar fates when moved from their homes to internment camps "inland."

The Aleuts' physical characteristics may have been responsible for their relocation. The Aleut and Eskimo words for Orientals translates to "like us." There are physical similarities. Perhaps for this reason the American government removed the Aleuts from their homes, for the stated reason of "protection" and the unstated reason: fear that they would fraternize and support the enemy.

The government chose Ketchikan as one of Alaska's Aleut relocation sites. Civilian Conservation Corps (CCC) barracks were available at Ward Lake, five miles north of the city. The CCC was a Depression-era version of the later Job Corps. The CCC boys had built Totem Bight park, worked at Saxman village park and when those projects were completed, left Ketchikan to join the military or other CCC units at work on the Annette military airfield in 1940.

The relocated Aleuts found themselves in 1942 in Ward Lake's rain forest of huge cedar, spruce and hemlock — Aleuts from the grassy, windswept Aleutian Islands who had never before seen a tree. Water quality and basic sanitation were substandard at the camp. It was off limits to civilians, and town parents warned their youth not to go to Ward Lake, a favorite picnic and play area.

Contact with communicable diseases took its toll and sickness broke out in the Ward Lake camp. There are Aleut families at rest together at Ketchikan's Bayview Cemetery. The survivors were returned to their homes after the Japanese were driven from the Aleutians in 1943. Some found their villages and churches destroyed and moved to different towns; others settled again in their homeplaces.

Ketchikan's Japanese-American population in December 1941 was listed in the newspaper at 42 — nine businessmen, eight other adults and 25 children. Not counted in that number were the sons of some of these families, already in the military and soon to be shipped overseas.

The Japanese-American units were the most highly decorated of the war. Charles Tatsuda was in Military Intelligence in the South Pacific and later in Japan itself; his brother Jim fought all the way across Europe and was wounded three times.

Ketchikan's Japanese-Americans were luckier than some from the West Coast states. They did not lose their homes and properties. Friends watched their properties for them during the three years they were interned in relocation camps "inland."

They did suffer the indignity. So did Ketchikan's young soldier Pat Hagiwara, who found himself in the unfortunate position of rounding up his hometown's Japanese-American residents for transportation to camps in Idaho and elsewhere. Hagiwara also returned from the war with honors.

Recently both the Aleuts and Japanese-Americans were paid reparations for their internment. This gesture — and time — may one day wipe out the memory of the fearful relocation and internment.

Photo by RCAF/Public Archives of Canada

A 115 (BR) SQDN Bristol Bolingbroke aircraft stationed at Annette Airfield, 1942-1943

Search and Destroy: Enemy Sub

(This brief story is excerpted, with permission, from a complete manuscript of the Cape Addington battle by Ketchikan historian Don ''Bucky'' Dawson.)

Not all the action of World War II was confined to strangely named South Pacific or Aleutian Islands remote from any urban setting. Far-ranging Japanese submarines prowled the Pacific West Coast from Alaska to San Diego, California. In fact, a number of non-strategic shore targets along the Canadian and U. S. Pacific Coast were shelled by surfaced enemy subs.

There were numerous reports of sub sightings in the Ketchikan district, many of which turned out to be whales or floating logs. But one sighting in July 1942 erupted into combat action, a sea battle only 80 miles from Ketchikan!

All U. S. and Canadian patrol vessels and aircraft were under orders to check out all boats, ships and planes they sighted. On July 6 Coast Guardmen from a boat patrolling the west coast of Prince of Wales Island were doing just that when they boarded a group of salmon trollers in a small inlet on Noyes Island. The fishermen reported that while trolling in open waters half a mile off the island's Cape Addington, they saw what appeared to be a sub's periscope about 100 feet away. They described the size and color and the bubbles created when it disappeared.

This information was quickly relayed to Ketchikan HQ, which passed it on to the Royal Canadian Air Force (RCAF) at Annette Island airfield just south of Ketchikan. The two closest depth-charge-armed patrol ships were alerted. These were the CG Cutter *McLane* and the Navy-requisitioned halibut schooner *Foremost,* painted wartime gray and outfitted for war duty. Both vessels headed for the sighting area. RCAF Bolingbroke bombers took off the following morning to conduct separate searches, but saw nothing.

Later that day another Bolingbroke took off for the day's final patrol search. Once over the general sub-sighting area, in spite of limited visibility in bad weather, the crew sighted churning waters and what appeared to be white smoke puffs below. The bomber banked and dived for the target and released a 250-pound anti-sub bomb. At 500 feet the crew was able

Courtesy of Captain N.P. Thomsen

Courtesy of Eileen Jones

LTJG Niels P. Thomsen (at left) and Ens. Ralph Burns (at right)

to discover a dark, cigar-shaped outline about 100 feet long running just under the surface. The men noted what might have been an elevation rudder but were unable to see a conning tower or deck guns.

The underwater explosion from their direct on-target hit sent a 60-foot plume of water into the air. The plane circled. No debris surfaced, no air bubbles or vessel track showed. But an oil slick two to four hundred feet in diameter appeared on the surface. The plane remained over the area for two hours, hoping for evidence of a kill, but were forced to return to Annette by fading daylight.

Both patrol ships that day were en route to the sub-sighting area, the cutter *McLane* in the lead, the *Foremost* delayed by bilge pump repairs. The ships were ordered to search for wreckage from the bomber's hit. They were over deep water but the chart showed a shallower area where a damaged sub might lie on the bottom to effect repairs. On the second day of the search the cutter picked up underwater engine noise, maneuvered into position and dropped a depth charge set for 300 feet. But it failed to explode.

Photo by USCG/National Archives

The 125′ U.S.C.G.C. *McLane* in white pre-WW2 colors

An hour later the cutter again began to pick up intermittent underwater noises of a zigzagging sub. After several hours and a change of direction, the cutter again picked up noises so loud that the Captain thought his own crew might be chipping paint in the engine room. The cutter dropped two depth charges and another pair 200 yards away. These were not duds. Big bubbles were reported seen not only by the ships but by Navy aircraft passing over.

The two ships came close together near the area of hit when the cry went up, "Torpedo!" First seen was a foot-high feather of water and then the yellow head and green body that passed harmlessly just under the bow of the cutter. Both ships headed in the direction from which the torpedo had come and where they now saw a periscope. The old *Foremost* dropped a depth charge and started into a turn.

Suddenly the *Foremost* seemed to be humping over some object, like going over a sandbar. The ship cracked the submarine hard, knocking her false keel eight inches off center. A smoke bomb was dropped to mark the spot and the *Foremost* hurried away. The cutter *McLane* moved in and dropped two more depth charges and a large oil slick appeared. The ships widened their search area, once again sighted a periscope and dropped more depth charges.

After this final assault, more oil came to the surface plus a hairy substance looking like rock wool — probably insulation. A buoy was placed on the spot. The ships cruised the area until one o'clock in the morning, able to see more oil and air bubbles surfacing. There were no more underwater sounds, no periscope, no sub coming to the surface.

The old *Foremost* limped into Ketchikan for repairs. Her slow speed hadn't allowed her to get far enough away from her own depth charge blasts, which had opened up some of her seams and added to the damage done by running over the sub.

A Navy review board at first had doubts that the sub had indeed been sunk. But the Navy Department made an official announcement October 30, 1943, crediting the sinking of a sub off Cape Addington as a combined effort of the RCAF patrol bomber, the cutter *McLane* and the YP-251 *Foremost*.

Flying Sergeant Thomas was the RCAF Bolingbroke's pilot, Pilot Officer Shebeski the observer and Sergeant LeLandais the observer/gunner.

Captain Niels P. Thomsen was commander of the *Foremost* and senior officer in charge of the sub action in July 1942. After the war he was commander of Base Ketchikan from 1950-51 and retired in 1952. Coast Guard Ensign Ralph Burns was commanding officer of the CG Cutter *McLane* and was awarded the Legion of Merit for his participation in the sub sinking. He retired as full commander in 1954 and died in 1988 at the age of 90.

At war's end the *Foremost* was returned to her owner Marcus Ness. As a fishing boat again, she was sold, resold and renamed and is suspected to have ended her days either sunk or unsalvageable on the rocks, possibly at Kodiak or perhaps in Sitka Sound.

The fate of the CG Cutter *McLane* is also uncertain. She was replaced in 1949 and was reported to be owned — if she survived an effort to prevent her scrapping — by a museum group in Chicago.

The Firebug Changes a Town

Fire has always been a major threat to Ketchikan. One of the first civic groups organized in the fledgling city at the turn of the century was the volunteer fire department. Fire fighters' responsibilities were serious in a town made mostly of wooden buildings perched on creosoted wooden piling. Adding to the fire hazard was the spark-spewing wigwam burner at the mid-town spruce mill.

Ketchikan suffered its share of fires in the first fifty years of its history, but it also was fortunate to have an alert and dedicated volunteer fire department which kept damage to a minimum. In 1959 the department earned a Class 4 fire insurance rating, a high honor for the firemen — and lower insurance rates for building owners.

But in the mid-1950s, a bewildering rash of fires had begun. The most serious of these was a July 15, 1956, fire that destroyed businesses on the Main Street end of the block between Mission and Dock. Lost were the 50-year-old Red Men Hall, the Coliseum Theater, Ketchikan Meat Company and Ralph's Liquor Store. (The area is a parking lot today.)

Fires were fought in other locations in the next four and half years. A January 1961 fire destroyed the Hunt Building on Front Street (at the location of today's Eagle Park.) But more, and worse, fires were to come that year.

Arson was suspected, but there was no vengeance rhyme nor insurance reason to the series of fires. Then firemen began to recall that volunteer fireman William H. Mitchell was always the first on the scene. Mitchell, however, was a personable young man from a nice family and was manager of a downtown business. There was no proof to support suspicions...although while Mitchell was visiting in California that spring of 1961, there were no more fires.

While Mitchell may have been a suspect, no one could anticipate a series of events during that year's Fourth of July celebration that culminated in major fires flaring up in three downtown businesses within a period of an hour and twenty minutes, in a city jam-packed with Independence Day celebrants. Nor would it be easy to believe that Mitchell arrived in town that day dressed in a woman's clothes for the express purpose of setting those fires — and then promptly left again.

Courtesy of Tongass Historical Society

Ryus block, January 1, 1958

At 3:20 p.m. July 3 the alarm was sounded for a fire reported at the Tongass Trading Apartments, above the Tongass stores at the corner of Front and Dock Streets. Firemen responded, a difficult task because Dock Street from Main to Front was blocked off for Fourth of July concession booths where an estimated 1,000 people were gathered.

Four minutes later, at 3:24 p.m., a fire was reported at the Federal Apartments, just three blocks away at the corner of Mission and Bawden Streets. More firemen responded.

While battling those blazes, another alarm was sounded at 4:40 p.m. at the Stedman Hotel, directly across the street from the first Tongass Trading fire. Ironically, it was the Stedman Hotel that had earlier called in the alarm for the Tongass fire.

A disguised Bill Mitchell, whom a subsequent news article reported as having trouble walking in high heeled shoes, strolled back to the Ellis air terminal and headed back south. He was dressed in what appeared to be a shirtwaist dress with a neck scarf, a shiny tan coat, a small hat with veil, matching handbag and shoes and wore sunglasses.

The Annette terminal called Ketchikan to report a man dressed in women's clothes. City police had a circular about a forger who sometimes disguised himself that way and notified the FBI in Anchorage. FBI agents were waiting for this passenger at Seattle, but he identified himself as Bill Mitchell — not the forger. So the FBI let him go. Mitchell continued back to California.

During the hours of his flight, firemen managed to contain the fires and save all three buildings, although affected businesses had some major repairs to make. The fires were set in the laundry/utility rooms of the buildings, using candles in glass candle holders as the tinder to set other material ablaze.

Mitchell turned himself in to California authorities and was brought back to Ketchikan within days. He was jailed and his bail was set at $150,000, at that time the largest bail ever levied in the State of Alaska.

Under questioning he had admitted setting not only the 1956 Red Men hall and 1961 Hunt Building and Fourth of July fires, but fires at the Marine Hotel that also damaged the Pioneer Hotel; the Betty King fire (King's home a tiny enclave in Pioneer Alley) that damaged the Union Rooms and Ketchikan Garage as well; the Senate Rooms fire; the Ketchikan Mortuary fire that involved the Bon Marche and Reagan Hotel, and the fire in the boiler room of the Mary Frances Apartments.

He was, of course, sent to prison.

In January of 1962, a course was offered in fire and arson investigation, attended by firemen, city and state police and the district attorney. The arson fires of the past were over and the city was prepared for the future.

(Information for this chapter from the files of Ralph M. Bartholomew, who was Fire Chief at the time of the Bill Mitchell fires.)

The Battle for Statehood

By Lew M. Williams, Jr.

At 4:45 p.m. June 30, 1958, the fire horn blasted in downtown Ketchikan. The Miners' and Merchants' Bank carillon bells rang 49 times. It signaled that the U. S. Senate had voted, 64-20, to make Alaska the 49th state. The House had approved the Alaska Statehood Act a few days earlier so the bill was on its way to President Dwight Eisenhower for his signature.

And Ketchikan residents were on their way to the ball park, Walker Field. Ironically, the field was named for Territorial Senator Norman R. (Doc) Walker, a Ketchikan pharmacist who had donated land to the city for the ballpark, but who vigorously opposed statehood.

An impromptu parade was organized at Walker Field by Captain Largent Miller, head of the U. S. Army Signal Corps unit in Ketchikan. A decorated fire truck led celebrating marchers to the corner of Mission and Front, near the Ingersoll Hotel and under a sign which read "The Canned Salmon Capital of the World."

There they heard speeches by Mayor Ed Winston, City Manager Bob Sharp, Alaska Chamber of Commerce President Charles Cloudy, Ketchikan Chamber of Commerce President Vic Guns, Junior Chamber of Commerce President Larry Franks, Territorial Senator Bob Ellis and Territorial Representative Bob Ziegler. Soldiers from the Alaska Communications System fired a 49-rifle salute.

The long distance communications system in Alaska was owned then by the U.S. Army Signal Corps. Later, ACS was transferred to the Air Force until sold to what is now Alascom, a private company.

After the ceremony, celebrants danced in the streets until midnight to music of the Pioneer Bar Band, the Ketchikan Daily News reported the next day.

Before Alaska was to become a state, Alaskans had to agree to three points of the Statehood Act in a primary election August 26, 1958: 1) accept immediate admittance as a state; 2) accept the boundaries outlined in the Act; and, 3) agree that the President had the power to withdraw a small portion of the northwestern part of the state for national defense.

Alaskans statewide approved the three points by a 7-1 margin. In Ketchikan there was a record turnout of 3,000 voters but approval was only 4-1.

It is easy to understand why Ketchikan's approval was less. Ketchikan was a divided community during the debate over statehood. The mining industry, the Alaska Canned Salmon Industry and other major businesses headquartered outside the state opposed statehood, fearing new taxes and loss of economic control. Ketchikan was Alaska headquarters for the salmon industry. At one time, nine canneries operated in the area which justified the sign "The Canned Salmon Capital of the World."

In post-World War II Alaska, the canned salmon industry wielded strong political and economic power. Mining had been crippled when gold mines were shut during the war as nonessential. Tourism, timber and oil development were yet to come. The salmon industry had prospered with prices and markets guaranteed during the war and with record salmon runs, especially in 1941 and 1949. It used some of that money to hire effective lobbyists in Juneau. One of those was W. C. Arnold, who was called Judge Arnold from his days as U. S. Magistrate in Hyder, a community supplied from Ketchikan. He had many friends in the canned salmon capital.

Military construction and opening of the Alaska Highway after the war increased the pressure for Alaska statehood. Its most active and vocal supporter was Territorial Governor Ernest Gruening. He traveled the Lower 48 and visited the nation's capital frequently promoting statehood. He also proposed that the Legislature assess more taxes to support the territory and eventual state government. Much of the new tax load fell on the salmon industry, including on its 212 fish traps.

Many in Ketchikan were involved in and supported the salmon industry and opposed Gruening, taxes and statehood. Others, especially fishermen resentful over fish trap competition, supported Gruening, statehood and taxing fish traps, preferably taxing them out of business.

The battle became so heated that Senator Walker, a Democrat like Gruening, spearheaded an unsuccessful effort during the 1947 legislative session to oust Gruening and have himself named governor. When Alaska was a territory, the president appointed the governor and secretary of Alaska. The Alaska Legislature had no power to replace the governor even though the Walker coalition tried to strip him of all power when they failed to have him replaced.

When Gruening's reappointment came up in 1949, Ketchikan attorney A. H. Ziegler headed a group of Alaskans who flew to Washington, D.C. to testify against Gruening at his Senate confirmation hearings. Gruening won confirmation after an equal number of northern Alaskans appeared on his behalf.

Statehood and Gruening supporters in the Ketchikan area were represented in the Legislature, countering Walker, by fisherman and Senator Andy Gunderson in 1945-46 and by Klawock businessman, Native leader and Senator Frank Peratrovich, 1947-49. Peratrovich went on to be a prominent state leader, serving as vice president of the state constitutional convention, as president of the First and Second State Legislatures and state chairman of the Democratic Party.

Legislators ran for office southeastwide when Alaska was a territory. At Ketchikan's political low point, no one from Ketchikan made it to the Senate in 1953. Only Republican William K. Boardman of Ketchikan served in the House. Senator Walker, after serving in the Legislature since 1933, was defeated when he sought re-election in 1948. Elected from Ketchikan in his stead was Dr. R. M. MacKenzie, a dentist, Democratic leader and strong Gruening and statehood supporter. MacKenzie was mentor to Oral Freeman, who went on to be a local and state political leader in the state's first 35 years. He still is politically active, having been appointed by two different state governors as a trustee of the Alaska Permanent Fund, a post he still holds.

Ketchikan had two opinionated newspaper publishers after the war and during the statehood fight. Sid Charles converted his tri-weekly Alaska Fishing News to the Ketchikan Daily News in 1947. Charles had been in the newspaper business throughout Alaska since 1904, eight years before the District of Alaska was made a territory. Becoming a territory also had been controversial. Charles opposed statehood for Alaska on the grounds that Alaska was too undeveloped to afford the cost.

The Ketchikan Chronicle was founded in 1919 and in the 1930s was Alaska's most influential and largest paper outside of Juneau and its Daily Alaska Empire. An Oregon newspaper man and Democrat, William L. Baker, purchased the Chronicle in 1944 and the battle was joined with

Charles. Baker supported Gruening and served as vice chairman of the Alaska Statehood Committee when it was created by the Legislature, at the urging of Gruening, to promote Alaska Statehood.

Heated editorial exchanges between Baker and Charles lasted until 1956 when the Chronicle went broke. Baker, who died in the late 1980s, always blamed his support of statehood for denying his newspaper advertiser support in Ketchikan. However, Baker had other business and personal problems that led to his downfall, as is attested to by the fact that the News prospered even though Ketchikan residents eventually supported statehood 4-1 and favored abolition of fish traps, an action not favored by Charles.

To measure the division over statehood in Southeast Alaska, it is important to note that of the four daily newspapers in the Panhandle in the 1940s and '50s, only the Chronicle favored statehood. The Juneau and Sitka papers were opposed along with the Daily News. Favoring statehood were the Wrangell and Petersburg weeklies owned by the Lew Williams, Sr. and Lew Williams, Jr. families, and the short-lived (1952-59) weekly Juneau Independent.

In the 1952 national election, Dwight Eisenhower was elected president as a Republican. That meant President Harry Truman's political appointees were out. Among those going out was Alaska's Governor Gruening.

Ketchikan's Doc Walker was no longer in the Legislature in the 1950s, the canned salmon industry was in financial decline, along with its fish runs. After Walker, Gruening and Baker were gone from the public scene, rhetoric moderated and support built in Ketchikan for Alaska Statehood. Ketchikan voters sent statehood supporter and pioneer aviator R. E. (Bob) Ellis, a Democrat, to the Territorial Senate in 1955, the only Ketchikan resident to serve in either house that year, as Republican Boardman had been the lone Ketchikan resident in the '53 session. Territorial legislatures of 16 senators and 24 representatives met every other year for 60 days, a limit set by federal law.

With Ellis and other pro-statehood lawmakers in control in Juneau, the Legislature called for a state constitutional convention to meet in 1955.

Ketchikan voters sent salmon troller W. O. (Bo) Smith as their delegate to the convention in Fairbanks. Also elected was Peratrovich from nearby Klawock, who later represented Ketchikan in the state Legislature.

The impact that fish traps had on the statehood battle is indicated by the convention's results. Only three ordinances were appended to the constitution. One called for an election to ratify the constitution. One called for the election of two Alaska-Tennessee Plan senators and an Alaska-Tennessee Plan representative to go to Washington, D.C. to lobby for statehood. It was the method Tennessee had used to win statehood. And the third ordinance called for a vote on the abolition of fish traps. The traps lost, even in Ketchikan, in a February 24, 1956 election.

In the election, the constitution was approved statewide by a 2-1 vote, sending Tennessee Plan congressmen to Washington was approved statewide 8,900 to 6,500 and traps lost by a resounding 6-1 vote. In Ketchikan, the constitution lost 675-769, the Tennessee Plan idea lost 496-909, but trap abolition was supported 1,185 to 275.

It's another irony in Ketchikan history that early-day Ketchikan merchant and businessman J. R. Heckman, whose name appears on area landmarks, is credited with inventing the floating fish trap. Early Indians made fish traps by blocking streams to catch returning salmon. Such traps were made illegal in 1889 by the first piece of legislation passed by Congress governing the new District of Alaska.

Heckman conceived the idea of putting traps at prominent points of land in Southeast, catching salmon as they swam by. Such traps produced a high volume of high quality fish relatively cheap because they fished 24 hours a day during a season opening, and without a crew. But the number of good trap sites was limited. They also were limited by U. S. Army Corps of Engineers and U. S. Department of Interior who granted permits and licenses.

By the 1930s, most trap site licenses had been acquired by salmon canneries headquartered in Seattle or San Francisco. Operating traps was cheaper for the canneries than buying salmon from seiners. Quality was often better because seiners took fish closer to the spawning ground. Traps created resentment among fishermen, especially when canneries used trap fish to keep down the price it paid fishermen for their catches. That resentment was channeled into a fight for Alaska statehood and its promised state control of fisheries.

Another irony is that while fish traps were owned by Puget Sound-based processors, such traps had been banned in Puget Sound in 1933.

After Alaskans voted on August 26, 1958 to accept the terms of the Alaska Statehood Act, Democrats won most of the seats in the November 25, 1958 general election to select a governor, a secretary of Alaska (now called lieutenant governor) and the First State Legislature.

The sharp division along party and economic lines had softened with the rhetoric. The community sent an entire Democratic delegation to Juneau, all of whom had been statehood supporters. Oral Freeman and J. Ray Roady were elected to the House and W. O. Smith to the Senate. Freeman was an outboard repair shop owner and former salmon troller and Smith was an active fisherman. Roady was a local businessman and Democratic party leader. He still is active in civic events, especially those of the Lions Club.

The only Republican who made a showing was Ketchikan Chamber of Commerce secretary, insurance man and former territorial legislator Boardman. He tied with Smith after ballots were counted. But the Democratic-dominated Senate seated Smith. Boardman had his day later in the state Legislature as House speaker.

The day after the U. S. Senate passed the Alaska Statehood Act on June 30, 1958, the Ketchikan Daily News' 87-year-old editor and publisher Sid Charles wrote: "The greatest historic change since Alaska was purchased from Russia will come when Alaska is admitted as the 49th state. We were opposed to admittance at this time because of the extra cost and scarcity of industries to support statehood. But it is up to all of us to get in and make statehood work. Our biggest present hope is for the favorable development of the oil industry."

How prophetic. The oil industry now provides 85 percent of the state government's revenue.

After a 55-year career with Alaska newspapers, Charles died 23 days after Alaska was officially admitted to the Union on January 3, 1959. It was the end of a major era in Alaska and Ketchikan and the beginning of a new one.

(Lew Williams, Jr. is a retired publisher of the Ketchikan Daily News. He joined the News as editor in 1966, after running newspapers in Petersburg and Wrangell since 1946. He and his family purchased the Ketchikan Daily News from the Charles family in 1976.)

Courtesy of Tongass Historical Society

First schoolhouse, Main Street, Ketchikan

Courtesy of Tongass Historical Society

St. Agnes Mission, 1896

Ketchikan School Days

Ketchikan's first school was an Episcopal Indian school, established in 1898, and located directly across from St. John's Episcopal Church (where the Ben Franklin store is today.) Classes were held in a cabin purchased from an Indian parishioner and were taught by Miss Agnes Edmond, a missionary and the first single white woman to live in Ketchikan permanently.

When Ketchikan was incorporated as a city in 1900, city fathers wasted no time in hiring a teacher and setting up a school. Classes were in full swing by 1901, taught by Mrs. Anna Hicks, wife of one of the town's dentists. Classes were held in the first Red Men Hall, also called the McIlravie Building, which must have stood just downhill on Main Street

Courtesy of Tongass Historical Society

"Ketchikan, Alaska — school of white children, March 1904."

from today's police station. By the end of the school year it became clear that more space was needed, so in August 1901 bids were called for a new school building to be built directly across Main Street.

The bid of contractors Canfield & Cornell was $1,377.50. Chris Hoover charged $180 for painting the new school white, with additional small charges for painting the cupola, porch, water closet and the coal house in the rear.

As school opened in the fall of 1901, classes were held at a second new school across Tongass Narrows on Gravina Island. A new community called Port Gravina had grown up there (where today's International Airport is located), around a sawmill built by Metlakatla interests. But fire destroyed the mill and store in the summer of 1904 and the families moved either to Metlakatla, Saxman or Ketchikan.

By 1904 the white schoolhouse on Main Street was unable to accommodate the increasing number of Ketchikan children, so a new and larger building was erected on top of Grant Street hill at a cost of $10,000.

Photo by Thwaites/Tongass Historical Society

Courthouse Hill, from Front St., Ketchikan

Photo by Thwaites/Tongass Historical Society

Main School under construction, 1926

The ground floor had two large playrooms. The second floor was divided into a large hall and three rooms, the smallest of which was the library. The other two rooms housed grades one through six and seated about 60 pupils. The third floor housed the seventh and eighth grades and the high school.

The old school building on Main Street was sold to the Roman Catholic Church in 1907, when Holy Name was established here.

By 1914 the school-age population of the city must have grown and Main School adapted to the need. A 1914 fire insurance map shows a large play shed, walled on two of the weather sides, and another large enclosed play area in the adjacent lot nearest the head of the Edmond Street stairs. Perhaps the ground floor of the new school, designed for playrooms, had been converted to classrooms.

About 1924 a two-year building program was under way to construct a new, concrete Main School building on the hill. The wooden school was torn down. Until the new building was complete, children and their teachers were farmed out to temporary classrooms in such places as the basement of the Methodist Church and in space offered by fraternal organizations.

As the West End neighborhood of Ketchikan grew rapidly during the first two decades of the century, a small school for grades one through three was opened at the top of Austin Street, just inside what was the city boundary at that time. Classroom space was so crowded there and at Main School that about 1920 the School District said it would have to begin charging tuition for students who lived north of the city limits.

Many of the students affected by the ruling were recent Norwegian immigrants, did not speak English and slowed the progress of classwork in the regular city school system. Their parents were not happy with the tuition plan. They petitioned for their own school district and their own school board and the Territory agreed to provide a school. Early in the '20s, the Charcoal Point School (named after the location, which was about where today's state ferry terminal is situated) was opened in Dynamite Joe's Roadhouse, vacated because of Prohibition. Students used only two rooms at first and then gradually filled the big building, studying in the old card room and bar, playing in the large dancehall and taking piano lessons on the player piano left behind when the roadhouse closed.

In 1925 the Episcopal Indian school on Mission Street closed its doors and the children were moved temporarily to the social hall of the Presbyterian church on Stedman Street (now the offices of KRBD public radio). The following year a new Indian elementary school on Deermount Street was completed. Graduates of that school generally went on to high school at the Wrangell Institute or Sheldon Jackson in Sitka, although a few chose to go to Ketchikan High School.

In 1927 the School District built White Cliff School for grades one through eight, relieving pressure on Main School. There would be no more public school construction for another 27 years.

In 1947 Alaska schools were desegregated and Native elementary school children enrolled in city schools. The government Indian school on Deermount Street was briefly used as housing for public school teachers. For a period of time in the late '40s and early '50s, the vacated building was used for Ketchikan school district seventh and eighth grades.

It was then bought by the Alaska Native Brotherhood and Sisterhood when they moved from their old hall on Guthrie Way, the stairway street behind the New York Hotel. In 1978 the old school/hall was torn down and the Ketchikan Indian Corporation headquarters built on the site.

It wasn't until 1954 that a new Ketchikan High School opened on the West End of town, with Main School remaining as an elementary school. When Valley Park Elementary opened, Main was vacated and was destroyed by fire in 1975. In 1961 Houghtaling elementary school opened, also on the growing West End. In 1965 Schoenbar Junior High School opened its doors, and in 1973 Valley Park elementary began classes, both near a new housing development on the southeast end of town.

In 1972 Revilla Alternative High School began classes in rented quarters and then in 1984 moved into its own new building across from Houghtaling Elementary School. In 1982 Clover Pass Christian School north of the city opened its doors. (Other denominational schools operated for varying periods of time.) In 1986 the school district's Point Higgins elementary was opened, at the far north end of Ketchikan.

A new Ketchikan High School is being built in stages to replace the 1954 structure on the same site as the present school.

Courtesy of Tongass Historical Society

Chief Fremont King (designated by "x")

Bucket Brigade to Career Firefighters

Ketchikan's volunteer fire department was already established some two months before the City of Ketchikan became incorporated August 18, 1900. D. Harris Smith, who was a city official in another capacity, was also named Fire Warden on that date. It was Harris who established the city's first organized fire fighting group, "the bucket brigade." To qualify for membership, you had to own your own bucket and be able to carry it full of water.

Fremont King was elected fire warden in 1902 and after a short period of time was succeeded by O. W. Grant for the rest of the term. Wardens King and Grant were faced with a booming community. Twenty-five new buildings were constructed in Ketchikan from the latter part of 1902 through 1903.

Fire prevention came into the picture as part of the department's organization when large barrels were placed on the roofs of the higher buildings to catch rainwater for fighting small fires. In 1903 a fire station was built to house equipment.

King was reassigned as warden in 1904 when, in May, the first equipment arrived, a chemical engine which provided a source of water under pressure for fighting small fires. This engine had two copper 35-gallon tanks, filled with soda water. It remained in service until 1918 and was used occasionally until 1923.

Courtesy of Tongass Historical Society

Ford T, 1914

Early maps fail to show a fire station or where equipment was housed, but it was probably on lower Main Street between Mission and Mill where City Hall and a tiny jail were located until about 1920. Then city hall moved farther up Main (the location of today's National Bank of Alaska's parking lot). That left the lower Main buildings to become a substantial fire station, until the present downtown fire hall was built in 1943.

It was also in 1904 that an electric fire alarm system was installed. Without telephones (which didn't come along until 1909) the four original street boxes were critical to early fire protection in Ketchikan. Later, ten additional boxes were installed.

Frank Bold was appointed fire chief in 1905. That year the department's first fireboat was purchased. Fremont King was chief-elect in 1906 when a hook and ladder wagon was hand-drawn.

Then in 1916, when Harvey Stackpole was chief, a Model A Ford fire truck was added to the department's equipment at a cost of $468.51. It was placed into service as Truck 1.

Lawrence W. Kubley was elected chief in 1925. Under his administration an American LaFrance pumper and a Seagrave pumper were purchased. They joined the equipment roster as Truck 2 and Truck 3. Truck 3 is still housed at the West End Station, and is affectionately referred to as "Grandma" by department members.

In 1928 a second fireboat was purchased with the department's own funds, and named for a past chief, Dale W. Hunt. The new fireboat was originally the first power seiner in the Ketchikan area, the *Ruth*. It was owned by August Buschmann, brother of Peter Buschmann, founder of Petersburg. The *M/V Hunt* saw 27 years of service, with its greatest test during the Standard Oil Company fire of 1952.

Engine 4, a 750 GPM four-wheel drive pumper, was purchased in 1952, when Stanley Adams was chief. In 1954 the *F/V Ethel* was purchased, when A.E. Brostrom was chief. She was renamed *The City of Ketchikan*, and later renamed the *H. V. Newell* after fire Captain Harry Newell, who

Courtesy of Tongass Historical Society

Practice, taken before 1917

Courtesy of Tongass Historical Society

Ketchikan Fire Department, 1932

died in a fire at the Smith Electric Company in 1955. The *H. V. Newell* was the only fireboat in the State of Alaska until 1983.

During the years Ralph M. Bartholomew was chief, from 1958 to 1964, an 85-foot American LaFrance ladder truck was added to the department's equipment, to Ketchikan's first ladder truck. Ladder 1-1 is still in active service in the downtown station. Chief Bartholomew's father, Ralph A. Bartholomew, joined the Ketchikan fire department in 1915, and the chief's son, Ralph G. Bartholomew, joined in 1971 — three generations of volunteer firefighters.

Roy Selfridge became chief in 1964 and during his term five career staff were added to the department and Engine 10, a new 1250 GPM pumper, was purchased.

Wally Winston became chief in 1968, serving until 1978. In 1976 Station 2 was built on the West End, replacing a temporary station at Austin and Tongass Avenue, used since 1954 during the construction of the Water Street and Tongass viaducts. An 85-foot Snorkle with a 1500 GPM pump was purchased for the new station.

The end of the 1970s was the end of an era, with the removal of all alarm boxes from the streets of Ketchikan. The noon fire whistle blast which startled hotel guests and by which residents set their watches was

Photo by Sixten Johanson/Tongass Historical Society

Cold Storage fire, 1945

gone. Also gone were the single blasts which meant an ambulance call, the double blasts which meant a fire call and the coded interval-blasts which located the box from which a call was made. The codes were printed inside the cover of the telephone book, so everyone knew the vicinity of the fire.

John Divelbiss became chief in 1978. The department bought a 1000 GPM pumper that year and another three years later. It was during this period, too, when the color of fire department apparatus changed from red to lime green, following a national trend to improve visibility and safety. During Divelbiss' tenure, employees hired as "maintenance personnel" would eventually change their status to "career firefighters."

Under Chief Gene Fisher, who was hired in 1982, the department's ambulance service began advanced life support services (ALS). Other progress was in a change to large diameter fire hose to improve supply capabilities and fireground efficiency. The *H. V. Newell* was replaced by the *Harry Newell* in 1986.

Chief David O'Sullivan, who joined the department in 1971 as a volunteer, worked his way up through the ranks to become chief in 1987.

(From information largely supplied by the Ketchikan Fire Department's "History" publication.)

The Ladies Library Club

In a small spiral notebook, saved in the files of the Ketchikan Public Library, are the penciled, undated notes of Mrs. Ray Hall, an early member of the Ketchikan Library Association. Her notes tell us that from the time Ketchikan was nothing but a few cabins and boardwalks, the ladies of the settlement had established a circulating library, and organized themselves into the Ladies Library Club.

The library by 1900 consisted of several shelves of volumes in a single bookcase provided by the club. The bookcase rotated, free of rent, from store to store, church to schoolhouse. Only women could be members of the library club, although men could be honorary members.

In 1902 the Ketchikan Land Company donated for library use a 50- by 100-foot lot and an old store building on Main Street near the corner of Dock Street (the site of today's National Bank of Alaska parking lot). The lot was adjacent to Mayor Mike Martin's corner house. A benefit dance

Photo by Harriet Hunt/Tongass Historical Society

Council Chambers and Public Library on Main Street

was held to raise money to clear the lot and put up a building. In 1903 a 20- by 40-foot building with reading room and book room was constructed, at a cost of $135.

Library club members paid dues of twenty-five cents a month and charged a small fee for the borrowing of books in their collection. With this money they bought more books and subscribed to magazines.

In 1907-1908 the City was deeded the library lot and building and agreed to pay a librarian's salary, twenty-five cents a day. The city in return temporarily used the library as council chambers and for elections. Then the City turned the library building a half turn to make room on Main Street for an almost identical 20 by 40-foot building for City use.

By 1908 the library club's name had changed to The Library Association. Minutes kept by secretary Harriet E. Hunt in that year indicate that the ladies needed either a new floor or a covering for the old one. The minutes do not indicate whether or not the ladies approached city council for this

Harriet Hunt

Courtesy of Tongass Historical Society

need, but there is mention of an offer from the City of "a suitable library room" elsewhere. The members, however, unsure of what "suitable" might mean, apparently found the $25 necessary to repair the floor themselves.

Additional bookcases were ordered from local carpenters, encyclopedias and reference books were gradually added to the shelves, magazine subscriptions widened and more books were bought. By 1911 "new membership cards were needed almost weekly." In 1912 a Professor Blake headed a benefit "entertainment" which raised $135.50 for a children's library.

In those early years a long-standing topic of discussion at the first-Tuesday-of-the-month meetings of the Library Association was whether or not to leave the library open when a librarian was not in attendance. This worry may have contributed to the Library Association's decision in 1936 to accept the offer of the City to move the library to the second floor of the newly purchased city utilities building on Front Street (now called City Hall.) In 1941 city council voted to pay all library expenses, and the fees for borrowing books ended. By 1944 it was reported that use of the library had gone up "66.66 percent" since the fee was discontinued.

In 1946 the original library lot was set aside as a site for a new library, when and if funds became available. The two old buildings there were still in use. One became the assay office. In 1953 one was used as a kindergarten classroom. In 1954 the brand new Ketchikan Community College was temporarily housed there.

Alaska's statewide celebration of the Purchase of Alaska Centennial in 1967 brought state and federal funds to the city which allowed the construction of the present library-museum complex on the banks of Ketchikan Creek. A "slum" area was torn down, streets realigned and the new facility was ready for occupancy.

On the library wall today is a plaque dedicated to the memory of Harriet E. Hunt and Marie C. Heckman, who represent all the pioneer women who made Ketchikan Public Library a reality.

Ketchikan's Hospitals

In Ketchikan's earliest days, doctors treated patients in their offices, and one turn-of-the-century doctor team is said to have worked out of a tent on Front Street until offices could be built. In a community of sawmills and miners, accidents were commonplace, and by 1904 there was an urgent need for a hospital.

St. John's Episcopal Hospital was opened in August 1904 in an Episcopal mission building vacated when the new St. John's church next door on Mission Street was opened. In 1905 a clergy house was built to the west of the mission and four years later it was converted to house the hospital. In honor of an East Coast donor to its construction, it was named the Arthur Yates Memorial Hospital for the donor's late husband.

In 1923 the Sisters of St. Joseph of Newark established a three-story hospital on Bawden Street, built by the Catholic Diocese of Juneau. The Episcopal Arthur Yates hospital then closed its doors in 1925.

The Sisters continued to operate the Bawden Street general hospital for more than 40 years. With Statehood in 1959, it became apparent that the outdated old facility could not meet new state licensing requirements. The Sisters requested a new hospital, and with citizen approval, a new facility was built on the West End of town. It was completed in 1963 and a nursing home wing added in 1968.

The 92-bed facility serves an area population of 28,000 people. With a staff of more than 250, the hospital provides the region with diagnostic equipment for mammography, CT scanning, ultrasound, nuclear medicine and traditional X-ray. It provides 24-hour emergency room physician care. There is nutritional counseling, rehabilitation therapy, a women's clinic, laser surgery technology and a substance abuse recovery center in addition to general health care services.

The Museums: Saving History

Ketchikan, incorporated as a city in 1900, was so busy "making" history as the town grew with the 20th century that it wasn't until 1961 that some of the oldtimers decided it was time to think about "saving" history. It was that year that the Ketchikan Historical Society was formed, spearheaded by Ketchikan's chapter of Beta Sigma Phi, with membership from the general community.

Ketchikan's first "museum" consisted of a donated display case and the lobbies and show windows of the community's businesses. The first collections included historical photographs, an old sewing machine, a collection of Ketchikan High School annuals and Indian artifacts including spruce root baskets, an adz, a sheep-horn spoon and stone tools.

One of the first items of business of the new society was to locate a permanent place to house the collections. In 1962 the municipal jail was moved to the federal building and the vacated space in City Hall was offered to the society for a museum. The windowless, 16- by 22-foot room became the first museum, with volunteer docents opening the room for a few hours a day.

In 1964, federal and state funds were made available to communities for the construction of public buildings or projects to commemorate the 1967 Alaska Purchase Centennial. The Historical Society successfully lobbied for a city-supported museum to share public library space in the planned Centennial hall exhibition center.

The site chosen for the new building was a parcel of land along the west bank of Ketchikan Creek fronted by Barney Way, a narrow avenue that was widened to become an extension of Dock Street. The warren of small houses and sheds on site were razed.

In 1967 the museum moved to its new location. Sixty percent of the main floor of the complex is library, the remainder museum exhibit area. In the lower level are staff offices, artifact storage space and the archives, which store government, business and industry records; diaries; tax rolls; voting registers; police blotters; newspapers; local phone books, annuals, maps, and a photo collection of 17,000 images of people, places and events from the 1880s to the present.

The rear of the Centennial building overlooks the lush greenery and historic Ketchikan Creek falls for which the town was named. The City commissioned the carving of the Raven Who Stole the Sun totem pole to grace the front of the complex.

In the years that followed the 1967 Centennial, a renewed interest in Alaska Indian culture spurred an inventory of all southern Southeast Alaska Indian village sites, documenting remaining totem poles for preservation. With the permission of Alaska Native populations, poles and fragments were moved to Ketchikan to be stored or displayed in a new city Totem Heritage center which opened in 1976.

The Heritage Center is located on the bank of upper Ketchikan Creek, across from City Park, on the edge of a traditional Native neighborhood. In addition to being a totem museum open for public tours, the Heritage Center is also a workshop center for Native culture classes.

THE WONDERS OF THE LAND

Misty Fiords National Monument

Misty Fiords National Monument is one of Ketchikan's chief visitor attractions, a spectacular and pristine scenic wilderness which can be reached only by boat or airplane — and sometimes weather prevents even that. The people of Ketchikan have long visited, explored and admired the attractions in their own backyard. But the Monument has only recently been "discovered" by the world, (although Captain George Vancouver sailed along the canal in 1793.)

The island on which Ketchikan is located is separated from the mainland by Behm Canal, a waterway that circles almost three-quarters of the island. The canal is the water highway to the undisturbed wilds of the Misty Fiords Monument, most of which is on the mainland.

The sentinel New Eddystone Rock with its colony of visiting seals marks the entrance to the much-visited scenic magnificence of Rudyerd Bay, the drowned U-shaped fiord scoured out by tributary glaciers to form the awesome Punchbowl Cove and its 3,150-foot cliff. Boat travelers, after a 50-mile run from Ketchikan, slowly cruise the silent waters of the cove and bay and view the old-growth stands of hemlock, spruce and cedar.

In the monument are hanging valleys, moraines, seagull rookeries, white sand beaches, cirques and tarns (bowl-shaped lakes), all visible from the air. Flying time is about 20 minutes one-way.

The Monument is managed by the U.S. Forest Service, which maintains recreation cabins and shelters in the Monument. There are also trails for hikers. A number of visitors each year use boat access to the Monument, carrying along kayaks to be launched for solitary exploring of the waterways and access to camp sites.

There is excellent fishing and hunting in season, with proper licensing. Lakes abound with Dolly Varden, char, brook, rainbow, steelhead and cutthroat trout. Misty Fiords also provides habitat for all five species of Pacific salmon.

The Forest Service recommends experience and caution in visiting the monument for extended stays, and advises familiarization with appropriate gear, with the possibility of contact with bears, and regional quirks of weather and water.

Photo by Schallerer/Tongass Historical Society

United States Forest Service vessel *Forester* in Walker Cove

Fish...and Wildlife

Ketchikan feels safe in calling itself The Sportfishing Capital of the World. In our waters are the wily king, coho, sockeye and chum salmon trying to outsmart fishermen, and in July and August so many pink (humpback) salmon that some charter boat operators guarantee a fish or no charge for the outing! There are also the huge and tasty halibut to be hauled in, the delicious red snapper and several species of cod and rockfish that find their way into the bottom of an angler's boat.

Since such big fish are out there in the salt water, most fishermen don't think about Ketchikan's many nearby lightly fished lakes and streams where several species of trout flourish unmolested. There's also excellent autumn steelhead fishing.

The salt waters of Tongass Narrows also provide a never-diminishing thrill each spring when pods of killer whales and gray whales frolic up the channel, heading for their summering grounds farther north. It's also possible to see, in waters fairly close to town, the occasional seal, sea lion, and porpoise. Beachcombers often startle mink, marten or otter.

There's a whole encyclopedia of strange and wonderful sea life clinging to the dock pilings right in downtown Ketchikan, brightly colored star fish, anemones and other exotic creatures.

Other wildlife, too, abounds — whether just for the thrill of seeing a bear or for hunting (in season.) The region's little "suitcase" deer can be seen in the woods, on the beaches and even swimming in the Narrows.

Swans can sometimes be glimpsed as they glide on forest ponds or lakes. Sandhill cranes may poke up their long necks on creek banks, even in town. Blue herons sometimes flap across the sky, looking like cartoon storks. Big, rusty black ravens, gleaming coal-black crows and noisy flocks of strutting seagulls can be seen scavenging almost anywhere. And in the trees are the songbirds serenading the mornings and evenings while jays scold and pilfer.

But perhaps the greatest thrill of all is an airshow by Ketchikan's many bald eagles. Sometimes they circle a cruise ship as if posing for the hundreds of cameras pointed their way. More often they can be seen scouting the Narrows for fish, perched on piling by canneries, and occasionally the lucky viewer or viewfinder will catch an eagle diving to the water with claws extended and returning to the skies with a flopping fish almost too heavy to carry. Wildife thrives in the wilds around Ketchikan.

"Gut Isle Flats"
by Terry Herda Gucker
(Dedicated to the memory of Jalon "Grandpa Jack" Gucker)

When I land in the silty sloughs of the Stikine, and see our duck shack tucked into the trees of Gut Island, I recall the many hunters who have come and gone before me, to this special place. Names like Jeff Anderson, Bob Sawyer, Ben Lund, Ray Roady, Shell Simmons, Quint Deboer, Tom Chandler and Reub Crossett come to mind.

But inside me, as I listen to the steady hiss of the Coleman lamps, the comforting burbling of the old oil stove, the muted cackle of the Canadas, and hear the haunting moaning of the Stikine wind, I think of Grandpa Gucker.

I think of all the times he sat in this rickety old chair by this round, oilcloth-covered table, drinking a shot of Schenley's whiskey with his hunting buddies. Looking out his many-paned window, making outrageous bets! Like winning this old whorehouse (which floats at high tide) in a poker game!

My eyes take in the bunk room lined with six bunks. Faded, curling, girlie pictures are stuck to the wall with chunks of masking tape. Grandpa's cracked, red-balled hip boots still hang from a nail in the corner. An old ski pole leans against the wall, his aid in walking the flats. A small table holds a saucer with a single candle in it. Yellowing Western paperbacks and wood matches lie nearby.

In the pantry are wooden shelves stocked with canned goods. Boxed groceries sit on the floor and a hearty supply of booze is stashed next to a jumble of decoys. A can opener holds the door in place! Nearly fifty years of tides have slanted the kitchen floor to a crazy angle. Pictures of bird dogs decorate the walls. And stuck in the frame of a stained mirror, hung above a chipped enamel sink, is a picture of Joe Louis.

A line with gloves, wool socks and towels stretches from above the dry-cupboard or above the warming oven of the stove. Directly above the water pail, a medicine cabinet holds an assortment of ancient grooming articles. Plus Sal Hepatica, mouthwash, Bay Rum aftershave and a green tin of Bag Balm.

Gearing up for the hunt, I heft my twenty-gauge from the gunrack. I picture Grandpa Gucker in his Filson and his old duck hat, goose and duck calls hanging from his neck, stuffing shells and decoys into his wooden shell-box and a flask into his hip pocket while yelling to his buddies to "Shut that goddamn gate!"

I glance once more at the table around which so many games have been played, so many whiskeys drunk, meals shared, stories told, and lasting friendships formed. I step out onto the sagging porch with its oil barrel, fuel tanks, and a sheet-covered water tierce. An outhouse and a weathered skiff are off to one side.

This is where he stood. Where he leaned his Parker. And patiently taught his two young sons to hunt. His seasoned hunter's eyes looked out over these very same marshy, golden flats, toward Little Dry and Big Dry channeled with sloughs, dotted with fallen trees and huge, uprooted trunks. Listening to the owl in the back trees, trees draped in pale green Spanish moss. I think of how he inhaled the same reedy smell of the marsh grasses (like the inside of an old Indian basket.) Tasted the same tangy rain-scented air, quickened to the same exhilarating essence of the hunt that I feel!

I feel so blessed to be here in this special place on these golden flats where Grandpa Gucker hunted. I feel so alive! Yet so at peace. For in my heart, I know his spirit hunts here still!

A sudden squall peppers the pot-holes in front of me like buckshot. Hiking my collar up around my neck, I shift my gun, step off the porch, and leaning into the bracing Stikine wind, I head out to the Christmas-tree-like landmark on the duck flats and the meadows far beyond.

The Amazing El Capitan Caves

Recently discovered caves on the northwestern tip of Prince of Wales Island to the west of Ketchikan have proven to be the first and third deepest caves in the United States. "Cavers," those people who spend as much time as possible exploring and measuring caves, discovered the El Capitan "Pit" and "Cave" in the summer of 1988. Their measurements were confirmed, and Alaska now holds yet another biggest-and-best record, a cave 598 feet deep.

At present these caves are not easily accessible tourist attractions. But that day may come. And visitors will be able to stand inside a cave and know that the surrounding rock is 400 million years old and the cave itself may have been carved by water 50,000 years ago. That's the most spectacular cave yet discovered, but there may be more. Where there's limestone and marble, there's a good possibility there are also caves.

Prince of Wales, a curious island, has some of the oldest geologic formations in the world. It probably was, at some time in the remote geologic past, an island in warm equatorial waters. Perhaps shifting continental plates brought the island to its present location. There is an old Indian legend that says at one time the island was a place of sunshine, vines and giant flowers.

There has not been time since the discovery of the caves to gather a great deal of archeological information. In the giant cave there is only the skeleton of a deer, shattered in a 600-foot fall. But there are other, shallower caves nearby that have cultural significance. These are closed until further studies can be made. How long ago man was there is not yet known. It could be anywhere from 100 years to 23,000 years ago or somewhere in between during the migrations of man across the Bering Land Bridge. Those things will be learned in time by the U.S. Forest Service, in charge of the cave site on Tongass National Forest land.

Aerial mapping by expert cavers brought the discovery site to light. The huge pits probably would have been noticed even if parts of the area hadn't been logged, but logging-exposed smaller pits indicated that this would be a rich area for cave exploration.

A number of disciplines are interested in this discovery.

Hydrologists are interested in studying the patterns of water through rock in cave formations; geologists in the types of marble and limestone forming the caves; archeologists in the evidence of early people; wildlife biologists in their specialty, and paleontologists in fossils.

The limestone formations indicate an ancient marine environment, shells built up over millennia. During one of the glacial periods the area was probably covered with ice, and the caves started forming as the glaciers retreated. Marble is "baked" limestone, so other forces were at work as well.

The El Capitan cave region is composed of thickness of about two miles, tipped on its side. There may be more exciting discoveries to come.